Hugh Caraher

A month at Lourdes and its neighbourhood in the summer of 1877

Hugh Caraher

A month at Lourdes and its neighbourhood in the summer of 1877

ISBN/EAN: 9783741193231

Manufactured in Europe, USA, Canada, Australia, Japa

Cover: Foto ©ninafisch / pixelio.de

Manufactured and distributed by brebook publishing software (www.brebook.com)

Hugh Caraher

A month at Lourdes and its neighbourhood in the summer of 1877

A MONTH

AT

LOURDES AND ITS NEIGHBOURHOOD

IN THE

SUMMER OF 1877.

BY

HUGH CARAHER.

LONDON:
R. WASHBOURNE, 18 PATERNOSTER ROW.
1878.

PREFACE.

I HAVE to throw myself upon the indulgence of my readers, and hope that they will forgive any deficiencies which they will find in the following pages. However they may view my efforts, I claim for myself an honest desire to bring before the public the great privileges obtainable at the blessed shrine of the Most Holy Mother of God at Lourdes, and, in the words of the poet-priest of Betharram, Pierre de Bastide, who gave up his soul to God in 1665, I humbly repeat:

"O Virgin! obtain for me, as the reward of my labours, not abundance of gold, nor precious stones, nor the vain glory of the world, nor soft delights, nor brilliant ornaments, but rather the gift of Divine Love, the light which shines in Heaven, and the unutterable joys of Eternal Life."

HUGH CARAHER.

LIVERPOOL,
  April, 1878.

CONTENTS.

INTRODUCTION.

BRIEF SKETCH OF THE APPARITIONS.—BERNADETTE SOUBIROUS.—NUMEROUS MIRACLES.—INVESTIGATION BY THE BISHOP.—MIRACLES PROVED.—POPE PIUS IX. APPROVES OF THE DEVOTIONS TO THE IMMACULATE VIRGIN AT LOURDES. - vii

CHAPTER I.

LIVERPOOL TO BORDEAUX.—INTERESTING CEREMONY AT THE CATHEDRAL.—BORDEAUX TO TARBES.—TARBES TO ST. PÉ.—CALUMNY ON THE SAINTE-PÉANS. - - - - - 27

CHAPTER II.

LOURDES.—WELLINGTON AND NAPOLEON.—THE CHURCH OF NOTRE DAME DE LOURDES.—PRESENTS FROM ALL NATIONS.—THE IRISH LAMP.—TOUCHING INSCRIPTIONS IN THE CHURCH. - 38

CHAPTER III.

GRAND CEREMONIES IN THE CHURCH.—PROCESSION FROM GROTTO TO THE TOWN.—A PERPLEXED IRISHMAN.—RIGHT REV. DR. MORENO, OF LOWER CALIFORNIA.—ESCAPES FROM HIS PURSUERS. - 50

CHAPTER IV.

VISIT TO PAU.—THE CHÂTEAU.—ABD-EL-KADER. QUEEN ISABELLA. — BEAUTIFUL CEMETERY.—ENGLISH CONFESSION.—RETURN TO LOURDES.—SOLEMN AND MOST INTERESTING CEREMONIALS.—BRILLIANT ILLUMINATIONS AND PROCESSIONS.—INTERIVEW WITH THE CURÉ PEYRAMALE. - 64

CHAPTER V.

SAINT AUGUSTINE AND CHURCH PSALMODY.—GREAT ASSEMBLAGE OF CARMELITE FATHERS TO HONOUR DR. MORENO.—MARKET-DAY.—FRENCH

AND IRISH MODES OF TRANSACTING BUSINESS.
—VISIT TO BETHARRAM.

CHAPTER VI.

BETHARRAM.—THE CALVARY.—WONDERFUL SCULPTURES.—THE CRUCIFIXION.—THE IMPENITENT THIEF.—MARY MAGDALENE.—THE PIE MATER.—RETURN TO LOURDES.—THE FESTIVAL OF THE ASSUMPTION.—GREAT PROCESSIONS AND ILLUMINATIONS. - - - - - 78

CHAPTER VII.

ARGELLES.—PEASANT PROPRIETORS.—ST. LUZ.—CURIOUS CHURCH.—WONDERFUL SCENERY.—BAREGES.—MINERAL WATERS.—THE PASS OF THE TOURMALET—SHEPHERDS ABOUT TO SHEAR THE SHEEP.—THE VALLEY OF THE CAMPAN.—GRIPP.—BAGNERES DE BIGORRE.—DEATH OF AN ACTRESS.—BURIAL RITES.—THE GREAT MARBLE WORKS OF M. GEREZUT. - - - 113

CHAPTER VIII.

THUNDERSTORM AT LOURDES.—THE NATIONAL PILGRIMAGE.—NUMEROUS MIRACLES.—AN IRISHMAN'S FAITH IN THE BLESSED VIRGIN.—A MIRACLE ON BOARD AN ATLANTIC STEAMER IN MID-OCEAN.—PIUS IX. SENDS THE GOLDEN ROSE TO LOURDES.—IRISH PRELATE PILGRIMS AT THE GROTTO.— RETURN HOMEWARDS.—TARBES.—LIMOGES: ITS CHURCHES.—ISSOUDUN.—PARIS.—VERSAILLES.—ROUEN.—JEAN D'ARC.—DIEPPE. - - - - - 131

CHAPTER IX.

PRESENTATION OF THE GOLDEN ROSE BY POPE PIUS IX.—INTERESTING CEREMONY.—SPEECHES OF THE ARCHBISHOP OF RHEIMS AND THE PAPAL DELEGATE.—PIUS IX. AND THE WATER OF LOURDES.—DETAILS OF NUMEROUS MIRACULOUS CURES. - - - - - 147

APPENDIX - - - - - 166

INTRODUCTION.

Brief Sketch of the Apparitions.—Bernadette Soubirous.—Numerous Miracles.—Investigation by the Bishop.—Miracles Proved.—Pope Pius IX. approves of the Devotions to the Immaculate Virgin at Lourdes.

IN the present day, when every one who imagines himself competent to instruct or amuse the public rushes into print, and contributes his share to the already overstocked literary market, some apology is due from me to my readers for my intrusion into the fields of literature. Had I consulted my own convenience, the following pages would have remained unpublished; but, yielding to the earnest persuasions of some friends who read the series of papers which I contributed to the *Drogheda Argus* newspaper, in the fall of last year, concerning the church and grotto of Notre Dame de Lourdes, I now issue this, my first attempt at book-making. It was also urged, that by giving in detail the best and readiest route by which the blessed shrine of the Mother of God can be reached, I should be doing a service to many whose devotional feelings might prompt them to pay a visit at the fountain of grace and mercy in the lovely valley of the Gave at Lourdes. As far as the latter is concerned, my readers will find in the Appendix ample information. I will add, that the pleasure derivable from travels in a strange country depends much upon the certainty with which a person can assure himself that he has in his hands a guide to point the way in which he should travel ; and the difficulties with which I had to contend I hope to remove from the path of such of my readers as may visit Lourdes.

Of the few works before the public treating of the wonderful apparitions of the Blessed Virgin at Lourdes, the most complete is " Notre Dame de Lourdes," published by M. Henri Lasserre, (1869), as an ex-voto offering for signal favours received. In this work full particulars are given of all the occurrences at Lourdes up to the date of publication, whilst Denys Shyne Lawlor's (1864) " Pilgrimages of the Pyrénées " has a chapter most piously and eloquently written on the wonder-working power which so many have received benefits from at the holy shrine. Canon Husenbeth (1870), Miss Caddel (1869), and Count Russell-Killough, in what they have written concerning Lourdes, have drawn all their facts from the noble work of Lasserre. The price at which Lasserre's book is published, as well as the language in which it is written, will preclude many persons whom my humble publication may interest from having an opportunity of perusing it. I will therefore draw upon M. Lasserre's great work for some facts relative to the apparitions, etc., at Lourdes, for the benefit of my readers; for this author, in giving his beautiful work to the public, was inspired with the hope that many would thereby be induced to hasten to Lourdes to honour Our Holy Mother, and through her powerful intercession gain graces for their own souls. Dare I hope that even my little efforts may tend to the like results?

One of the most painful facts which Catholics experience in travelling is the infatuated bigotry which stares them in the face in every page of the pretended guide-books wherever mention is made of objects or places hallowed by the early recollections of the saints and martyrs of the Catholic Church. That from amongst the numerous educated Catholics who yearly travel on the Continent of Europe, no one has been found to supply the antidote, by giving a true guide, is a surprising, and, I must say, a discreditable fact. Whilst lamenting that such is the case, I hope that some competent person will take this matter in hands, and give to Catholics who may travel abroad a book which will indeed be a guide to them.

As, no doubt, many who may peruse these pages will not have an opportunity of visiting the thrice blessèd shrine of Lourdes, I will, for their especial benefit, give a succinct account of the miraculous apparitions—eighteen in all —which our Blessed and Holy Mother deigned to make, and some of the happy results flowing therefrom.

Towards the close of the year 1857, François Soubirous, a humble man, and his family lived in a poor dwelling adjoining a mill, by labouring in which he earned a scanty support for his family. Soubirous had four children: two sons and two daughters. The eldest of the family was named Bernadette, who from

Introduction. xi

her infancy was subject to illnesses. A neighbouring peasant in the sweet vale of Bartrés undertook to nurse and bring up Bernadette for the small sum of five francs a month ; which, small as it was, François, her father, found it difficult always to pay, having often to make up the stipend in labour. The kind family into which Bernadette gained admission became very much attached to her. When she was able to go out into the fields, her employment was to tend the lambs and goats as they browsed upon the herbage of the valley. Bernadette grew up in the love and esteem of her benefactors, and her health was considerably improved. Being now in her thirteenth year, her parents thought the time had arrived when their daughter should return home to be prepared for the most important act in the life of youth, the worthy reception of her First Communion. The good nuns of the convent of St. Vincent de Paul lovingly undertook the training of the young shepherdess, and little did they think what a glory to their Order she would one day be, by becoming a member of their community. But, how inscrutable are the ways of God !

February, 1858, saw the Lourdois making

ready to hold their annual civic festival of Shrove Tuesday; but whilst they and their houses were decked out for the feast, there was one amongst them whose hearth was desolate, for no fire burned thereon. This was in the home of Soubirous. Bernadette's mother sent her children out along the banks of the Gave to gather some brushwood, wherewith to make a fire. The two daughters of Soubirous, accompanied by a neighbour's little girl, Jeanne Abadie, went forth on their mission. The children got upon an island, formed by the junction of the Gave and Merlasse, and approached a spot opposite the rocks of Massabielle. A mill-race separated the children from the rocks; and as the mill was then undergoing repair, the water was shallow in the mill-race. Bernadette's sister and Jeanne Abadie took off their sabots, and crossed over to the rocks, where, in a natural cave, some brushwood was found. Bernadette was anxious to go across also, but as she had stockings on, she asked her companions to throw a few large stones into the water, that she might step over without wetting her feet; but they replied, "Do as we have done, and come across." Bernadette leaned against a tree, and commenced to take off her shoes and stockings, when her ears were saluted with the sounds of the *Angelus*, which came from many a convent and monastery, on the hills and the valleys, and fell sweetly upon her ears. Instinctively the young shepherdess, as was her wont, fell upon her knees, and took out her rosary, which she always carried with her, and commenced to tell her beads as she repeated her prayers.

As she was thus engaged, a mighty wind swept over her head, which greatly startled her. She looked up, and saw that the lofty poplars under which she knelt stood perfectly motionless. She was mistaken; no wind had disturbed their branches. Again she prayed, and again was she startled by a whirlwind! Raising her head, and looking in the direction the wind had taken, she saw, in a niche above the cave in the rock, a figure which filled her with awe—a life-size representation of the Holy Mother of God, surrounded by all the effulgence of heavenly glory! The lovely apparition smiled sweetly on the humble shepherdess, and beckoned to her to cross the stream. Having done so, she inquired of her companions if they had heard or seen anything strange.

They answered that they had not. The bundles of sticks were gathered up, and the three girls directed their steps homewards. Noticing something strange in the manner of Bernadette, her sister and Jeannie urged her to tell them if she had seen or heard anything. Under a promise of secrecy, Bernadette related what she had heard and seen, when at once the two girls said, "It must have been the Mother of God." Thus out of the mouths of babes had wisdom spoken. Childlike, the girls no sooner reached their homes, than they took their mothers into their confidence, Bernadette's saying it was only a fancy, and should not be thought any more about. The soul of Bernadette had been too solemnly touched by Divine Love to give way to the suggestion of her prudent parent. Other visits to the grotto were made by her, and still the Holy Virgin was there to console her. The visits of Bernadette became noised abroad; and her parents, fearful of injurious consequences happening to her, forbade her to go to the grotto. The clergy of the parish, apprehending that a scandal to religion might arise from the alleged apparitions, did all they could to dissuade the people, who now began to flock daily to the grotto, from

Introduction.

going there. Monsignor Laurence, bishop of the diocese, prohibited any of his clergy from countenancing the stories told, and from being seen at the grotto, and all that prudence could do to prevent any scandal arising from the alleged occurrences was done by those having charge of the ecclesiastical affairs of the diocese. Notwithstanding these measures, the faithful flocked in increasing numbers to the shrine, as they termed it, of Our Holy Lady.

Bernadette, although restrained by her parents' wishes, felt herself impelled, by some agency, to her inexplicable, to visit the grotto; and on each of the eighteen visits upon which the Divine Mother of God appeared and spoke to her, she was the more firmly convinced of the truthfulness of the apparitions. The good and holy curé of Lourdes, M. Peyramale, talked the matter over with Bernadette; and, as a test of the truth of the apparitions, he told her to ask the Lady to make the wild rose-tree, which grew around the niche, put forth its blossoms. Bernadette, on the next visit, conveyed to the Blessed Virgin the curé's request. The HOLY VIRGIN smiled at hearing the wish of the curé; and, inviting Bernadette to come closer to her, she pointed to a corner of the grotto, telling her to scrape away some of the earth, and wash and drink of the water she would find there. Bernadette did as directed, and, behold, a stream of water answered to the efforts of the tiny fingers of the little shepherdess, as did the rock to the wand of Moses, when leading his people towards the Land of Promise. The curé also commissioned Bernadette to ask the apparition what was her name. In answer to this the Holy Virgin, holding a rosary in her blessed hands, said, "*I am the Immaculate Conception!* Tell the priests I wish a church built here, and to have processions come here."

Here was a visible fact. The apparitions were only vouchsafed to Bernadette, in the midst of countless crowds ; but the springing forth of the fountain was too much for the sceptical to account for. Officialdom must now step in to put a stop to such vagaries, as they termed the occurrences at the rocks of Massabielle. All the military and civil authorities now put forth the means at their disposal to discredit the statements made ; and as, despite the injunctions of the bishop and clergy, the people persevered in going to and praying

Introduction. xvii

at the grotto, they (the Government authorities) would see if such nonsensical proceedings could not be put down. Vain men! How impotent are your reasonings against the decrees of God! Proclamations were issued, forbidding any one to trespass upon the lands around the rocks of Massabielle, as it was property belonging to the government of the town. Barriers were put up, and police officers detailed to see that no one challenged the orders given. Nay; those men in authority even went so far as to arrest Bernadette, as one primarily responsible for the manifestations which were being made. The mayor questioned her, the police magistrate sought to confound her; but as there was no evil in the child, truth triumphed over worldly machinations. Failing to confound her, they sought in their malice to circumvent her liberty by placing her in a lunatic asylum at Tarbes; and for this purpose a committal was made out. The Curé Peyramale heard of this matter, and, although he had most prudently abstained from identifying himself with Bernadette's proceedings, saw that the time was come when the pastor of the flock should shield his charge from the wolves who sought to devour it.

2

He saw the mayor, and told him, "If you invade the sanctuary of the home of Bernadette, to take her forcibly away, you must first pass over my body." Glorious recollection for the writer that he had the great privilege of enjoying the society of this holy servant of God, who has since passed away to his eternal reward in the kingdom where the Immaculate Mother of God sits beside Her Divine Son for all eternity.

The barriers were still around the precincts of the grotto, when one day a gentleman approached, and attempted to push his way through. He was accosted by a police-officer—I use the name police-officer as better understood than the French name, gendarmerie—who asked his name. "My name," said the stranger, "is Louis Veuillot." The talented editor of the Paris *Univers* soon had a passage made for him. Where in France is not that name respected and feared? Whilst the altercation was going on at the barrier, a lady passed through, and, whilst kneeling at the grotto, offering up her petitions to the Mother of Mercy, an officer approached her and told her she must not pray there. He asked her name, so that he could have her cited before the mayor. "I am," she answered, "the wife of Admiral Bruat, and governess to the Prince Imperial." It is needless to add that Louis Veuillot and Madame Bruat were allowed to finish their devotions.

Whilst all this manœuvring on the part of the government officials was going on, there lay in the house of Jean Bouhohorts, at Lourdes, a little boy labouring in the agonies of death. The child's eyes were already glazed, and his breathing was hardly perceptible. Madame Ducouts, a good neighbour, stood beside the crib of the dying boy making a shroud to enwrap his body previous to its burial. The mother of the boy, absorbed in the grief which alone a mother can experience, would not leave the room at the request of Madame Ducouts. Madame Bouhohorts seized the boy, enveloped him in her apron, and declared her intention of bringing him to the grotto, and bathing him in the water. "Croisine," said her husband, "if our Justin is not dead, you will surely kill him." "What matter," answered the wife, "whether he dies here or at the grotto? Let me go to implore the help of the Mother of God." She left the house, and ran to the grotto.

When the crowd saw her approach, they thought that she was out of her mind. Reaching the grotto, she threw herself on her knees, and laid her petition at the feet of Mary. Full of faith, she plunged her boy into the water, where she immersed the seemingly lifeless corpse for the space of fifteen minutes. The people were horrified at the woman's conduct. She took the child out of the water, put him again into her apron, and hastened home. When her husband saw the child, he said, "You see he is dead, he is frozen." The rigidity of the child's limbs justified the father's exclamation. Croisine put the boy into his crib and covered him with clothes. After a time she leant down over the crib and had the inexpressible satisfaction of noticing him breathe. Two days afterwards the young boy, who from his debility never was known to walk, was seen running about the streets of Lourdes! Again, Louis Bourriette, whilst working in a quarry, met with an accident which caused him to lose the sight of one eye. The best medical skill available was had recourse to, in the hope of getting relief, but not alone were the doctors powerless to restore the sight of the injured eye, their efforts were unable to retain the sight of the other one. Scarcely able to distinguish night from day, Bourriette mustered resolution to send his daughter for some of the water from the grotto, which he no sooner applied to his eyes than the sight was instantly restored. Going out into the town, he met Dr. Dozous walking along the street. He accosted the doctor, and declared that his sight was miraculously restored through the intercession of the Blessed Virgin, and the use of the waters of the grotto. Dr. Dozous examined the man's eyes and tested their visual powers. Having had Bourriette for some time as a patient, he openly declared, amidst a crowd of people who had gathered around, that no human agency could have effected such a cure, and he felt compelled to admit the fact of the cure being miraculous.

The authorities still remained obdurate, and would not remove the barriers placed around the grotto. His Grace the Archbishop of Auch, and some other eminent Catholics, went as a deputation to the Emperor Napoleon, then staying at Biarritz for the benefit of sea-bathing, and having laid all the known particulars about the apparitions at Lourdes before the

Emperor, the latter telegraphed to the authorities at Lourdes to withdraw from the precincts of the grotto, and remove all obstructions which they had placed in the way of the people visiting the sacred shrine. Miracles continued to be almost of daily occurrence; and as it was in the early days of Our Lady's Blessed Shrine at Lourdes, so is it to-day.

The time at length arrived when the bishop of the diocese took steps to show how much of truth there was in the wonderful occurrences taking place at Lourdes. For this purpose his lordship issued a pastoral, in which he made known his desire that a commission of inquiry should investigate all matters connected with the grotto. His lordship said, "Three classes of persons have appealed to our decision, but each with different views. First, there are those who, refusing all examinations, see nothing in the events at the grotto and in the cures attributed to the waters of the fountain but superstition, trickery, and fraud. It is evident that we cannot adopt the opinions of such persons à *priori* or without serious examination. Their journals at once raised the cry of superstition, imposture, and bad faith; they affirmed that the occurrences at the grotto had their origin in sordid interest and culpable cupidity, and thus have wounded the moral sense of our Christian population. To deny everything, to throw suspicion on the best intentions, is, we allow, a very easy way to get rid of difficulties. The denial of all supernatural action is but the revival of a superannuated school, which would end in the abjuration of the Christian religion, and lead men to follow in the wheel-ruts of the infidel philosophy of the last century. We Catholics cannot take counsel with those who deny to the Almighty the power of exceptional interference with the general laws which He has established for the government of the world—the work of His own hands, nor can we enter into discussion with them upon the supernatural character of particular facts, inasmuch as, beforehand, they proclaim the impossibility of the supernatural altogether. Does this mean that we refuse a full, sincere, conscientious, and enlightened discussion of these events? Certainly not. We desire it with all our energy. We wish that these events should be submitted to the severest rules of examination which sound philosophy admits; and in order to pronounce whether these occurrences are supernatural and divine, we desire that men specially versed in the science of mystic theology, of medicine, physics, chemistry, and geology, shall be summoned to their investigation, and we desire, in order to ascertain the truth, that no means of science and learning shall be omitted."

This commission, so carefully selected, commenced their labours on the 17th of March, 1858, at Lourdes, under the presidency of the arch-priest, Canon Nogare. After a long and searching scrutiny into the events at the grotto of Massabielle, all the witnesses being examined under the obligations of an oath, they made their report to the bishop, in which they say:—"Of the thirty extraordinary cures examined, six were deemed capable of a natural explanation; nine most probably supernatural, but yet possible under the influence of some unknown force of nature; fifteen declared to be absolutely miraculous, and perfectly impossible except through the direct intervention of God." The bishop had this report laid before him. He did not immediately take action upon it, but allowed three years to pass away before returning to the subject, when he ordered the commis-

Introduction.

sioners to re-assemble, and to visit each of the fifteen cases which they had pronounced "miraculous," to see if the cures were of a permanent character. All the persons were still found healthy, for they had had no return of their maladies. His lordship, feeling himself justified in speaking authoritatively on the question at issue, sent forth a pastoral letter, dated the 18th January, 1862, in which he said: "We pronounce that Mary Immaculate, Mother of God, did really appear to Bernadette Soubirous on the 11th of February, 1858, and on the following days, to the number of eighteen times, at the grotto of Massabielle, near the city of Lourdes; and that this apparition possesses all the characters of truth, and that the faithful are justified in believing it with certainty. We humbly submit this our judgment to the judgment of the Sovereign Pontiff, who is charged with the government of the Universal Church." The Holy Father, in a Bull issued on the 4th of September, 1869, confirmed the decision of the Bishop of Tarbes. On the 8th of December his lordship the Bishop of Tarbes canonically established a confraternity in honour of the Immaculate

Conception, and on the 14th of February, 1873, the Holy Father raised this sodality to an arch-confraternity, which he enriched with many special indulgences, one of which is that any person visiting the church of Our Lady at Lourdes, once a year, gains 200 days' indulgence, which can be used as suffrages for the souls in purgatory.

In 1864 his lordship the Bishop of Tarbes laid the foundation-stone of the basilica of Nôtre Dame de Lourdes in the presence of a vast multitude of people.

The present appearance of the basilica and grotto will be found very imperfectly described in the following pages. I had intended to give here some interesting particulars of the miraculous occurrences at Lourdes in the latter part of August and September, but must defer those to Chapter IX.

I now leave the work to the kind consideration of my readers, humbly asking them to overlook the many shortcomings they will find in its pages.

A MONTH AT LOURDES.

CHAPTER I.

Liverpool to Bordeaux.—Interesting Ceremony at the Cathedral.—Bordeaux to Tarbes.—Tarbes to St. Pé.—Calumny on the Sainte-Péans.

It might be deemed presumptuous in the writer to give a detailed narrative of his travels in sunny France, but his object in visiting that country was that he might pay his loving respects to the Blessed Virgin at the privileged shrine of Lourdes, where, through her great intercession, so many miraculous manifestations of the power of God are being almost daily made. In these days of rapid travelling hardly a spot exists which has not been explored and described; but, as scarcely any two travellers see the same object from the same point of view, I hope to make my impressions of what I saw and heard during my sojourn in France as interesting as possible.

Guide-books are at the service of all who leave their own country for foreign lands; but I must confess that as far as Catholics are concerned, Murray and others are not reliable, and I shall have occasion to notice some of the errors into which some of those guides (?) have—I hope unintentionally—fallen.

As many of my countrymen are visitors at Lourdes, and as others, no doubt, will follow, it may interest those who contemplate a visit if I point out the best and shortest way to reach that most interesting and highly favoured place. For this purpose I shall give my narrative the form of a diary, and by this means hope to prevent the confusion which otherwise might arise in my description of ceremonies which, although in many particulars similar, took place under different auspices and on different occasions. One word more personal to myself. I prefer giving my name, so that I may be held responsible for any statements which I shall have to give, and not from any spirit of egotism.

July 25th.—Left the river Mersey at 7 p.m., by the Pacific Company's mail steamship *Sorato*,* in company with a fair number of

* *See* Appendix.

A Month at Lourdes.

passengers, some bound for the west coast of America, some for Buenos Ayres, others for Spain, and not a few for Lourdes. Among the latter were some of the grandchildren of two of the most remarkable men who trod Irish soil during the past hundred years—O'Connell and Charles Bianconi. With a fine evening and a noble ship, all was joyousness on board. Night coming on, the cabins were resorted to, and an early peep at the next day's sun was anticipated. But, alas for human hopes! Very few of the happy passengers were to be seen on deck next day. That terrible scourge, the *mal de mer*, had paid a visit to the pillows of many on board, and as a consequence few of the voyagers could venture on deck the following day.

July 26th.—With fine weather, we had a good view of the rock-bound coast of Cardiganshire, and at 8 p.m. we were off the Land's End, coast of Cornwall, the gallant barque skimming the waves, scarcely making the least uncomfortable motion.

July 27th.—In the forenoon entered the dreaded Bay of Biscay, but the water was as smooth as a millpond. How different from its angry state when poor G. V. Brooke spoke his last few words ere the ill-fated London took that brilliant Irishman to the bottom of the sea; or later, when her Majesty's war-ship *Captain* was, along with the hundreds she had on board, engulphed beneath its waters. After passing through the bay, we espied the *Cotopaxi*, belonging to the Pacific Company, homeward bound from Valparaiso, with the mails and passengers from the several ports on the Pacific coast. We stopped to exchange our Liverpool pilot. Not the least pleasing incident of this day was the witnessing of the glorious orb of day taking leave of us in all its added splendour, to seek repose in the bosom of the mighty Atlantic. As the sun hid himself from us in the west, the pale clear light of the moon shone out to welcome us to the shores of chivalrous France.

July 28th.—At 2 a.m. dropped our anchor in the Garonne. There we lay till 6 a.m., when we tripped our anchor and steamed to Pauillac, a distance of some 35 miles up the river towards Bordeaux, where we were landed at 10 a.m., the *Sorato* not going any higher up the Garonne. We left Pauillac in a river steamer, and, after a pleasant sail, landed at the quay at Bordeaux at 2 p.m.; thus making the passage from Liverpool to Bordeaux—650

A Month at Lourdes.

miles—in 60 hours, deducting time lost in stoppages. Bordeaux is a fine city, having some noble buildings and spacious squares, and umbrageous boulevards. It is the second city in France, and its shipping exceeds that of any other French port. Had time permitted, a day could be well employed in visiting some of the many interesting sights which are to be found in Bordeaux. The magnificent cathedral of St. André will repay the visitor for his trouble in going to see its many interesting objects. This cathedral is specially interesting to English travellers, as having been erected by their progenitors, when Bordeaux was in the hands of the English, who held it for three hundred years. Richard II. was christened in St. André's, and the marriage ceremony of Louis XIII. of Spain to Anne of Austria, in 1615, was celebrated before its high altar. The church of St. Michel's is richly adorned with sculptures and paintings by the old masters, and has a gorgeously decorated interior. Adjoining the church is an octagonal tower 403 feet high, from the top of which a grand view of the city and surrounding country can be had. There are few finer sights to be had than that which the bridge affords, as you cross the Garonne. The church of St. Severn is a most interesting building, erected in the fifth, and added to in after centuries. There are other objects in the church worth inspecting, among them a bas-relief of Clement V., who, before being raised to the papal dignity, was Archbishop of Bordeaux, offering up the Holy Sacrifice. The Theatre, one of the finest in Europe, and in which the Government held their deliberations when driven out of Tours in 1870, is really a noble structure. The Museum, with its sculptures and paintings, and the Bourse, must not be passed over without a visit. The Botanic Gardens are really deserving of notice, the more especially so, as the omnibus fares are reasonable, and the route so beautiful and interesting. Hotel accommodation is befitting the character of the second city in France—good tables, and reasonable charges. For persons making but a short stay, the Hôtel du Commerce fronting the church of Nôtre Dame, will be found very handy from its central position.

July 29th.—Visited the church of Nôtre Dame, a large and beautifully decorated structure. The carvings in stone upon the front entrance will well repay inspection. At 10 a.m. attended High Mass in the cathedral of

A Month at Lourdes.

St. André, where the ceremonies were carried out in an imposing manner. A procession of the priests and choristers went round the church singing hymns, some of the clergymen playing upon brass instruments, whilst the choir and organ gave the alternate verses in a solemn manner. The music was Gregorian, and from the numerous voices of the priests, choristers, and congregation, the lofty roof was made to resound with heavenly melody. There is a clock-tower attached to the cathedral, having a gilded statue of St. André on its summit. Visitors would do well to ascend to the platform of this tower, from which lofty position a splendid view is had of the city, its churches, palaces, parks, and bridges, as well as a good glance at the wine-fields of Medoc and Charente. After dinner, left Bordeaux for Tarbes, 154 miles distant. The country, after leaving Bordeaux, is a perfect level for nearly one hundred miles; and from the sandy nature of the soil, it would appear that at one period the sea must have covered its surface. A pine forest, in which wolves and bears are said to exist, covers the ground, and several of the trees are tapped for the purpose of extracting resin from them. The railway, for the distance named, neither goes under nor over a bridge, so level is the country. Excepting at a few woodmen's huts, inhabitants are not many in the forest. After passing Morceaux, the country becomes more interesting. Large tracts are covered with maize, the tall stems of which, of a bright green, and capped with flowers, give the fields a very beautiful appearance. Luxurious fields of potatoes, whose various coloured blossoms enliven the scene, testify to the absence of the dreaded "beetle." The corn crops are gathered into the farmyards, and the numerous fruit trees and vine plants bear their fair share of the luscious products. Arrived at Tarbes, we found the town full of soldiers, they having been concentrated there for summer drill and rifle practice. This town is the chief depôt for the training of the French cavalry, and very large studs of horses are kept there. Tarbes is the chief residence of his lordship the bishop of the diocese in which Lourdes is situated. It is a very handsomely situated town, close to the foot of the Pyrenees; and persons desirous of visiting the fashionable baths and pleasant town of Bagneres-de-Bigorre, can break their journey at Tarbes, from which they can reach the former place in an hour. On their way they have a good view of the lofty Pic du Midi (11,500 feet), and also the beautiful valleys through which the rivers Adour and Gave pursue their meandering courses towards the sea.

July 30th.—Left Tarbes for Lourdes at 7 a.m., where we should have arrived at 8 a.m.; but, owing to an oversight, we were carried past the station to Saint Pé, a distance of nine miles further towards Pau. Although this was to some extent a disappointment, it proved a very pleasing incident in our journey. Saint Pé is a village situated on the right bank of the foaming Gave, and is surrounded nearly on all sides with verdure-clad hills, some of whose tops are covered with perpetual snow. The place is remarkable, in that it possesses a very extensive diocesan seminary, in which 260 students are located, for whose instruction and guidance there are sixty resident priests. At the time of our visit there was a clergyman superintending the erection of a theatre in the playground, and several groups of young men were conning their parts in the drama under the shades of the tall and wide-spreading walnut trees surrounding the open space, whilst others were practising the choruses incidental to the performances which in a few days were to take place, as vacation time was close at hand. Saint Pé must have been at one time a thriving town. It has a large square, surrounded by a colonnade, in which business was transacted, and the politics of the day discussed by the city fathers, whose heads now lie mouldering in the neatly kept little cemetery. In the centre of the square is a representation of the Sacrifice on Calvary. The town is now principally inhabited by nailers, and stocking and linen weavers. For the first time in my life, I saw yarn being spun from the distaff, at which several old women were employed, as they sat in friendly chat at their doors. I examined some of the yarn, and not being altogether unacquainted with the article, I must say that the thread spun by this primitive contrivance was of a very fine description, and of a perfectly uniform character. The village hostelry prepared a good dinner for me, my wife, and a clerical friend from Kildare. After partaking of it we left the town, having spent five pleasant hours in its rustic streets. I must notice one of those slanders which the compiler of Murray's Hand-Book, and to which

I have already referred, has tried to fasten upon the residents of Saint Pé. He says that "the place is chiefly inhabited by beggars." I assert, in justice to the simple and industrious inhabitants of this Catholic village, that although I and my party traversed all its streets during the five hours we spent there, not a single individual solicited an alms from us. The French are a keen, observing race, and, from the foolish idea which they possess of English wealth, some of them are rather importunate in pressing their claims upon the bounty of travellers who hail from the golden land; nevertheless, the fact is as I state, and I make Mr. Murray a present of his gratuitous misrepresentation of the people, who, ignorant of his charge, can be courteous and obliging to strangers without playing the part of whining mendicants. I fear that in this instance, as in others, I shall have occasion to notice that the religion of the people is not acceptable to their critics.

CHAPTER II.

Lourdes.—Wellington and Napoleon.—The Church of Nôtre Dame de Lourdes.—Presents from all Nations.—The Irish Lamp.—Touching Inscriptions in the Church.

JULY 30TH.—The glorious sun has tipped the points of the mountains with his golden rays as I wend my way to the church and grotto of Our Lady of Lourdes. Early as is the hour—5 a.m.—crowds are going to and returning from the grotto. As publications, easily procurable in Great Britain and Ireland, are before the public, I will not stop here to recount all the occurrences which took place at Lourdes during the eighteen days on which the Blessed Virgin appeared to the little shepherdess, Bernadette Soubirous. It will suffice to say that Bernadette was the daughter of an humble miller, whose necessities caused his daughter to go along with other children to gather firewood in the vicinity of the rocks along the Gave, and that on the 11th of February, 1858, whilst so employed, the Mother of God appeared to and conversed with her. How Bernadette's constancy was tried by the cautious prudence of the curé and the bishop of the diocese, how her parents were annoyed by the intrigues of the local government authorities, and how the apparitions were finally admitted—all these matters are, as I have said, of ready access to all who may feel an interest in studying the books published. The Holy Father, by his Brief of the 4th of September, 1869, raised the sodality of the Immaculate Conception at Lourdes to an arch-confraternity, and the churches of the crypt and basilique of Nôtre Dame were erected ; hundreds of thousands of pious souls have flocked hither to gain spiritual and bodily comforts. As the basilique of Nôtre Dame at Lourdes is a church most worthily erected for the glory of God and the honour of Our Blessed Lady, it is fitting that I should say something of its many beauties and rich adornments ; but perhaps I should first say a few words about Lourdes itself before going any further in my narrative. Lourdes, then, is a town in which stirring scenes were enacted during the days of the Crusaders, and, later still, in the wars of the nineteenth century, under the Iron Duke. Wellington had his quarters here for a time when on his way to Spain, and early in this century the French had Lord

Elgin a prisoner in its fortress. The fortress still stands sentinel over the valleys and passes of the Gave and the Lavedan ; but, beyond a few soldiers who look after its proper keeping, no troops are now stationed there. Lourdes is 170 miles distance from Bordeaux—the nearest route for persons leaving England ; and travellers need be under no apprehension of not finding sufficient hotel accommodation, good and reasonable, and honestly conducted, at Lourdes. The beautiful valley of the Gave is peculiarly appropriate for inspiring the most devotional feelings. The ever-murmuring music of the river, as it tumbles over its rocky bed, the quantity and variety of the trees growing around, the lofty Pyrénées standing, in their towering height, like sentinels to guard the peaceful scene—all go to form an enchanting *tout ensemble* not easily to be met with, and drew from an enlightened Protestant visitor the expression, "I must say that if the Virgin appeared here she showed a rich appreciation for the beautiful in nature." The basilique stands upon the left bank of the Gave, its lofty spire is 300 feet above the level of the river. The style of the church is a mixture of the Roman and Grecian modes of architecture.

All that the skilful artist who designed the sacred structure could do in the space at his disposal has been done, and few of our modern churches can compare favourably with this noble pile. The basilique stands over the beautiful chapel of the crypt, and, externally viewed, the whole appears but one church. The crypt chapel is a very neatly constructed building; its many columns rendered necessary by the superincumbent church, give it quite an interesting appearance. It has five chapels in which the Holy Sacrifice is daily offered upon their altars. Immediately beneath the crypt is the grotto wherein Our Blessed Lady appeared to the little girl, and in the opening of the rock, a sort of natural niche, where she stood, there is now placed a marble statue, life-size, of exquisite workmanship in the art of sculpture. This statue is the gift of two pious sisters of Lyons—the Madlles. Lacour. The grotto has a railing placed before it, but the gate is left open during the day for visitors to go inside. Day and night hundreds of wax candles, the votive offerings of the faithful, burn before the sacred shrine, and kneeling crowds of devotees throng the neatly arranged space between the grotto and the river. Adjoining the grotto are baths for both sexes, supplied with water from the miraculous fountain. No charge is made for the use of the baths, neither is any money taken for the water given to visitors. I mention this because, since I returned from Lourdes, I saw it stated in a public journal, that the priests at Lourdes were making an article of commerce of the water. Outside the grotto there is a rustic pulpit, which is frequently used by clergymen to preach to the pilgrims whom they accompany from home to Lourdes. That the church and grotto might not be encroached upon, his lordship the Bishop of Tarbes has secured a large tract of land surrounding the sacred spot. Ascending the steep hill which separates the grotto from the basilique, we get upon the platform upon which the portico of the church stands, and, looking through the lofty centre doorway, the interior of the church presents to the view a scene of the most surpassing grandeur and loveliness. From floor to lofty ceiling—150 feet high—from every coign of vantage flags and banners are depending, rich in all the materials of textile fabrics, displaying the various hues of the rainbow in their golden and silver emblazonments. Most of the nationalities of the Christian world have their appropriate ensigns floating under the spacious roof of Nôtre Dame de Lourdes. It would be deemed incredible were I to say how much wealth was devoted to the production of the flags. As an instance, the splendid flag from the Catholics of the United States of America, presented in 1873, cost $6,000. Beautiful as this flag is, many more in the church far exceed it in costliness. Amongst the nations which paid homage to Our Lady of Lourdes, Ireland, ever faithful and devoted to the Blessed Mother of God, holds her proper place. Thanks to the pious Catholics of the diocese of Clonfert, the flag of Ireland proudly bears itself aloft in the gilded throng, in all the glory of emerald sheen and brilliant gold. No flag in the church so soon rivets attention as the one from Clonfert. Made of green silk, on one side enwreathed with golden shamrocks, the "Harp of old Ireland" holds its honoured place, whilst on the obverse, similarly surrounded, stands a faithful representation of one of the crosses at Monasterboice. At the top of the flag is the word "Clonfert," and at the bottom, "Irlande." The beautiful flags brought to Lourdes by Father O'Dowd and his fellow-pilgrims, representing the Catholic associations of Canada, in green and gold, and the brilliant flag of Maryland, in all its striking colours in stars and stripes, are placed within the sanctuary. Rich and rare as are the numerous flags, their cost bears but slight comparison to the other votive offerings displayed around the interior of the basilique and upon its altars. Here are to be seen precious gems, the once coveted adornments of their possessors; stars and other decorations, which Emperors and Kings had placed upon the breasts of warriors and statesmen; jewel-hilted swords, now laid in peaceful repose, the keen edges of which opened the way to fame and honour to the men who bore them in the deadly combat; the golden mitres of departed prelates, and the many costly articles of gold which once were used at the altar; innumerable heart-shaped lockets of gold and silver, in each of which is enclosed some pious petition to the "Comfortress of the Afflicted" —these stud the walls of the church and the several chapels, like so many brilliant stars in the firmament. In a niche immediately over, and belonging to the tabernacle is placed a casket containing five precious jewels, valued at £3,000, the munificent gift of the Duke of Orleans. Wonderful as is the charity to and love for the Temple of the Lord, as shown by these costly offerings, there are not wanting others which, in their touching simplicity, appeal strongly to the souls of the onlookers. Here in one of the chapels is a bridal wreath of flowers, of which the young bride despoiled her brow, that she might, even in this humble manner, pay homage to Her whose compassion for the family at Canaan, at the wedding feast, induced her Divine Son to work His first miracle. A poor sea-tossed mariner, thankful for mercies vouchsafed to him, having neither gold nor silver to spare, presents the labours of his hands, and the very interesting model of his good ship "St. Anne," as she approached the harbour of Bordeaux, finds a place within the church of Our Lady at Lourdes. The Holy Father, too, has remembered Lourdes. The most cherished *souvenir* at Lourdes is the gift of the Pope. At the time of the Papal Jubilee the Catholics of Spain sent a deputation to congratulate his Holiness, and brought as a present golden palms. In 1877 a pilgrimage came to Lourdes from

Italy; and the Holy Father, to show his veneration for the shrine of Our Lady, made the Italian pilgrims the bearers of the "palms" as his offering to Lourdes. The "palms," I need hardly state, coming as they did from Catholic Spain, and for the Father of the Faithful, are a singularly and costly combination of the precious metals and of brilliant gems. On high festivals they are placed upon the High Altar in the basilique.

Ireland's gift of a silver lamp, richly burnished with gold, costing £300, holds the premier place in the sanctuary—immediately in front of the tabernacle. This beautiful specimen of Irish genius and workmanship stands out conspicuous amongst its numerous attendant lamps, all of befitting grandeur for such a temple, but all immeasurably dwarfed into comparative insignificance by the splendour of the "Lamp of the Children of Saint Patrick." The devices wrought upon the several compartments of the lamp clearly proclaim its origin. "The Harp of old Ireland," the Irish wolfdog, the Celtic cross, St. Patrick, and other richly chased ornaments, lend added charms to this magnificent votive offering. "Erin's immortal Shamrock." is profusely displayed upon this "Lamp of the Sanctuary." Here I find myself compelled to digress for a moment, whilst I endeavour to arouse the feelings of those patriotic and pious Catholics in Ireland, who aided the good Father Kinane of Tipperary in placing the "Lamp of Ireland" in the basilique of Nôtre Dame de Lourdes. In the midst of shining lamps within the sanctuary, the "Lamp of Ireland" seldom sheds its rays upon the scene! How comes this neglect? Surely the people who kept the lamp of Kildare's holy shrine burning for 1,000 years will not permit the Irish lamp at Lourdes to remain unlit. If no provision has been made for the supply of oil for the lamp, I hope my drawing attention to the fact above stated will cause this to be remedied. I cannot say that my experience of La Belle France, wherein Ireland is concerned, altogether pleases me. Two years ago, when travelling across the plains of Landen, I looked in vain for any monument to show that Sarsfield fought and died there for the honour of France, and when his heart's blood was fast ebbing out on that ensanguined field drew from him the expression, "Would that this was for Ireland." Again, when looking through the picture gallery of the

Palace at Versailles, in which all the chief battles of France, from the earliest times to the day when the present ruler of Germany was proclaimed Emperor within its walls, are portrayed, Irishmen are left out in the cold. Fontenoy—glorious for Irishmen's valour—is there displayed, but no sign on the broad expanse of canvas is given to inform the onlooker that an "Irish Brigade" took hand or part on that glorious conflict.

In the eighteen chapels which are placed around the basilique are fixed slabs of marble divided into spaces, on which are inscribed the thankofferings of the faithful who have had the privilege of visiting the shrine of Our Lady, or have gained graces through her intercession. I will give a few of these inscriptions:

"RECONNAISSANCE À MARIE SOUVENEZ-VOUS
SAINTE MÈRE,
DES FAMILLES KIERNAN ET COLEMAN
DU COMTÉ LOUTH,
IRLANDE."

"AMOUR ET RECONNAISSANCE
D'UNE IRLANDAISE
1875."

"UNE MÈRE: RECONNAISSANCE
A. N. D. DE LOURDES, POUR UNE
CONVERSION ET DE GRÂCES OBTENUE."

A Month at Lourdes.

> "JE DOIS A MARIE IMMACULÉE
> LA CONVERSION DE MON PÈRE."
>
> "A MARIE IMMACULÉE, AMOUR ET RECONNAISSANCE,
> POUR LA GRACES BONNE MORT TU ELLE
> A ACCORDÉE A MON PÈRE."
>
> A MA MÈRE BIEN AIMÉE
> N. D. DE LOURDES, ETERNELLE RECONNAISSANCE
> MARIE VICTOR HENRI BALDIT, A ÉTÉ
> M RACULEUSEMENT GUÉRI PAR L'EAUX DE LA FONTAINE
> DE LOURDES, ET LA FAMILLE RECONNAISSANTE
> AISSANTE DEPOSE AUX PIED DES AUTELLES
> DE TRES SAINTE VIRGIE MARIE."

When it is remembered that eighteen chapels in the basilique and the five in the crypt church are all lined from the floor to the height of six feet with marble slabs, and have inscriptions prompted as above, the number of persons who have thus recorded favours received must be considerable. Persons from the most remote parts of the four quarters of the globe have testified thus the obligations they owe to the holy shrine of the most Blessed Mother of God. What other portion of the church will afford other suppliants the means of recording their thanks I cannot see, unless the expansive floor be utilised for this purpose.

CHAPTER III.

Grand Ceremonies in the Church.—Procession from Grotto to the Town.—A Perplexed Irishman.—Right Rev. Dr. Moreno, of Lower California: Escapes from his Pursuers.

THE high altar of the basilique is a very imposing structure. It is enclosed on three of its sides by a lofty screen wrought in bronze, which is of elaborate workmanship. From the ceiling of the church depend a large number of chandeliers, each holding some fifty candles. The chandeliers, when they require to be replenished, are lowered by means of chains carried through the ceiling and worked from a floor above the same. The mode of lighting these candles when in their lofty position is an ingenious one. The candles in each chandelier are connected by a thread of gun-cotton, and a string hangs for a considerable distance down below the chandelier, having a connection with the strings referred to. The vergers, having a long wand upon which a waxlight is placed, touch this string, and instantaneously a thousand lights shoot into existence. To anyone who has witnessed the sudden display of light thus given, it will be a long time before its effects fade from his memory. The church is supplied with two organs, one of which is placed behind the high altar, and is generally used at Mass and at Vespers. The other stands in the organ loft over the porch at the entrance to the building. This latter is a most powerful instrument, and is only used on occasion of high festivals. Its magnificent appearance at the distant end of the church adds considerably to the beauty of the interior of the sacred edifice. As already stated, the basilique of Nôtre Dame de Lourdes is placed on a spur of the Pyrenean range, and viewed from the opposite side of the Gave forms a pleasing object in the landscape. The hills rise sharply upon its southern side to a considerable distance. On one of the hills there is built a granite altar of a very substantial character, and having upon the right hand a lofty Crucifix, the Figure upon which is over twelve feet high. Far away up the mountain, standing upon a broad plateau, is placed another cross, which, from its eminent position, is visible for leagues around. The altar and crosses are the gifts of the pious Celts of Bretagny, who charged themselves with the cost of their erection, and left them as a *souvenir* of their pilgrimage to Lourdes in 1875. The Priests in charge of the mission at Lourdes intend to make this mountain a calvary as soon as their means enable them to do so. At present their hands are tied for want of funds. Besides this, the numerous works now being carried on by the Fathers fully absorb their time. They have just completed the building of a house for the use of the bishop of the liocese, and also a place of residence for all other bishops who may visit Lourdes. The house stands in beautifully laid out grounds. Between the bishop's house and the basilique there is approaching completion a large dwelling for the accommodation of the fourteen clergymen attached to the church and grotto. There is also a large hospice being built, which will soon be ready to receive pilgrims. This building will be an acceptable residence for the many humble devotees who make an effort to visit the grotto of Our Lady The hospice will be under the loving care of the good Sisters of the Seven Dolours, who will be able to supply accommodation to over two hundred persons during their stay at Lourdes Another good work is also in hand. The Priests are building a refectory alongside the river, where persons who come for a day to Lourdes can have their food cooked and served up to them free of all charges. Besides all these undertakings, the Fathers are engaged in building a bridge at tne junction of the Gave and the Merlasse, which, when completed, will make a straight avenue from the railway station to the basilique and grotto, whereby the distance will be much less from the former to the latter than is now the case, and the necessity of going into the town to reach the church will be avoided. The Sisters of the Capuchin Order are also having a handsome convent and conventual church erected. All these undertakings give employment to a large number of tradesmen and labourers, and as there is a cessation of work at these undertakings on the Sunday, the example is having a good effect in causing other workmen to observe the day in a better manner than has hitherto been the case in this part of France. The visitor at Lourdes would do well to pay a visit to the convent of the Immaculate Conception, which stands about a mile lower down on the banks of the river. In the grounds of this convent there is a representation of the Virgin Mother of God, which is of surpassing loveliness. It is painted in relief on an oaken plank, and impresses one as that of a life-size figure. It is almost impossible to view this statue and not be persuaded that the Blessed Virgin is looking at you, and is about to address you, so realistic is the work of the artist. In this convent ladies visiting the grotto can find accommodation at reasonable charges. Immediately opposite the basilique there are two extensive conventual establishments : one belonging to the Benedictine, and the other to the Carmelite Order of Nuns. Lourdes proper has convents of the following Orders of Nuns : Little Sisters of the Poor, Poor Clares, Sisters of St. Vincent de Paul, Immaculate Conception, Carmelites, and Benedictines, and large schools are taught by the Sisters who reside therein.

To-day a pilgrimage of 600 persons came from Bezieres. The pilgrims were in charge of the Curé of Sainte Madeleine, who had several other Priests with him. Solemn Vespers and Benediction was given at 2 p.m., and a sermon preached by the Curé. In the evening the pilgrims again assembled at the grotto, recited the rosary, and sang the Litany of the Blessed Virgin. The Curé once more preached, using the rustic pulpit of the grotto for the purpose. His impassioned and fervent eloquence made a wonderful impression upon the vast assemblage congregated before the grotto. The shades of night were fast falling, the murmurings of the fierce Gave were hushed into quietude by the earnest outpourings of the preacher, whose auditors showed by their feelings how deeply their souls were touched whilst the privileges of the Mother of God were descanted upon by the eloquent Curé. After the sermon the whole assemblage sang the *Magnificat,* and as the vast body of heavenly music resounded through the valley, no heart present could resist the impulse of grace thus brought home to it. A torchlight procession was now formed, and the pilgrims moved from the grotto towards Lourdes. Having reached the public square, the *Magnificat* was again sung, and a young clergyman stood up on a raised position, and delivered an address in fervid eloquence to the crowd, who, before dispersing to their respective lodgings, gave three hearty cheers for "The Pope," for "The Church," and for "France." Well, indeed, did the editor of the *Journal de Lourdes* express himself—" What would Voltaire say to such proceedings in the public places of a town in France? The people have torn down their former idols, for Our Gracious Mother of the Grotto has conquered all hearts." There was one thing which impressed itself forcibly upon my mind—namely, the beautiful harmony produced by the singing of the devotional hymns by the peasantry of France. Part-singing is taught in all the schools by the religious teachers, and the degree of perfection attained in psalmody by the people shows how carefully they have been trained.

July 31st.—Heard Mass at the Basilique, the celebrant being the good Parish Priest of the town of Newbridge, Kildare, Ireland—Father Martin Nowlan. The rev. gentleman was one of my companions from Liverpool, and he left to-day for Paris. Our acquaintance was but of short duration, but it was long enough to show me that in Father Nowlan the "Old Soggarth Aroon" is still to be found amongst the priests of the Catholic Church in Ireland. When Father Nowlan left me, I met another good Irishman in the person of James Talbot, of Clonmel, Tipperary. As the faith and devotion of the Irish Catholics found a true exemplar in my friend Talbot, a slight sketch of the man and his endeavours to reach Lourdes may not be uninteresting to my readers. James Talbot had an affliction which deprived him of the full use of his right side, and hearing of so many wonderful cures at the grotto at Lourdes, he resolved to make a visit to the Virgin's shrine at that distant place. A few friends supplemented his own scanty means, and this heroic confessor of the Faith of Ireland went upon his mission of hope. Taking passage from Waterford, he arrived at Bristol, thence to London, Newhaven, and across to Dieppe. Talbot found himself at length in Paris. Instead of taking the nearest route for Lourdes, he took the train for Toulouse, mixing up the places in his mind. When he got to Toulouse, he endeavoured to find the grotto, and for this purpose spent the better part of two days in his fruitless search. On the second day he saw a Catholic priest, to whom he tried to make himself understood, but could not fully do so. This priest asked him if he was " Un Angleterre." Talbot's only French word, " Irlandaise," acted as a talismanic spell upon the feelings of the clergyman, and after a little more effort to understand each other, the priest finding that Lourdes, and not Toulouse, was the Irishman's destination, took him to the railway station, and sent him on his journey rejoicing. Arrived at Lourdes, he had no great difficulty in reaching the grotto, where he made the acquaintance of one of the best of Irishmen, and a true son of St. Ignatius of Loyola, Father Carton, S.J. This worthy and highly esteemed priest is not unknown, I believe, in Drogheda and its neighbouring counties; and when I state that as soon as he discovered my friend's impecunious position he charged himself with the cost of his maintenance whilst at Lourdes, and also provided him with the means of reaching Liverpool on his way home to his native Clonmel, where he has safely arrived. All who know Father Carton will say, "It's just like him." I saw Talbot this morning, at the grotto, and made his acquaintance. Hearing me converse in English with a lady from Calcutta he at once warmed to me. In the afternoon I again saw my friend at the grotto: indeed, he was as much a part of that sacred spot during his stay as were the railings which enclosed it. This time he seemed to be labouring under some perturbation of spirits, the cause of which I soon found out. Whilst I was away, two men came to

A Month at Lourdes.

the grotto, both of whom conversed together in the English language. These men interested Talbot, who listened to their conversation. One of them was an Irishman; the other, his brother-in-law, was a Frenchman, from Paris. The Irishman was dilating upon the powers of the Blessed Virgin, and recounting how graces had been conferred through her great intercession by pilgrims who had visited the shrine before which they stood. The Frenchman sneeringly spoke of the Mother of God, and pitied the credulity of those who believed in such stories. Talbot's blood began to course rapidly through his veins, and in utter grief he turned away from the grotto, lest his feelings of resentment might gain the mastery of his patience. It was whilst he was labouring under these feelings that I met him, and learned their cause. I said, " Never mind him : it only shows his deplorable want of faith." "True for you, sir," said he ; "but what vexed me most was that I could not knock him down and kick him for falling. Two things only prevented me : I could not explain to the people why I did it, and the spot was too sacred to cause any turbulence in its precincts. I am sure had

I done so the Lord would forgive me." Whilst narrating his story to me his eyes flashed with fire, and were I that Frenchman, I would prefer meeting Talbot anywhere than in the neighbourhood of Slievenamon or Galtimore. Talbot being a staunch adherent to the principles taught by Father Matthew, I had no chance of soothing his perturbed spirit by a glass of the product of the generous vine. This evening, after another visit to the grotto, the pilgrims from Bezieres took their departure for their distant homes, after having edified all who witnessed the depth and sincerity of their two days' devotions at the shrine of Lourdes.

August 1st.—This being the vigil of the great Feast of Portiuncula, large numbers flocked to the basilique to gain the indulgences attached to the feast. Monsignor Marincy, Bishop of Dulma and Vicar Apostolic of Brownesville, Texas, arrived at the grotto to-day. There was Benediction at two o'clock; and a sermon by a Franciscan Father from Lyons. The preacher, who is the author of several works of a religious character, delivered a very eloquent discourse upon the Festival of Portiuncula, and on the merits of the seraphic founder of the Franciscan Order. Many of the Franciscan Fathers from the neighbouring convents were at Lourdes during the day, and assisted in the confessionals.

August 2nd.—Early at the basilique, where hundreds who had travelled overnight were assembled around the numerous confessionals. Masses commenced at five o'clock, and were continuously said up to eleven o'clock. The Right Rev. Dr. Marincy was a considerable time occupied in giving Holy Communion at the nine o'clock Mass. Sermon and Benediction again at 2 p.m. Although rain fell most of the day, it had very little effect upon the thousands who eagerly performed the prescribed devotions, and it was a remarkable feature in the attendance at the church that a great portion belonged to what the world calls the upper classes.

August 3rd.—To-day a noble confessor of the Faith appeared at Lourdes in the person of his Grace the Right Rev. Dr. Moreno, Bishop of Lower California, who came to return thanks to Our Lady of Lourdes for favours received through her intercession. Dr. Moreno had more regard for the honour of God than for the mandates of the Government of Lower California. They, not being able to bring the prelate over to their way of thinking, had the wickedness to lay their sacrilegious hands upon the Lord's anointed minister, and cast him into prison, from which, like another Peter, he was miraculously delivered. His lordship belongs to the Carmelites, and to-day we had a great many of the same Order who had come to Lourdes from Tarbes, Bagneres de Bigorre, and other places, to honour so eminent a Bishop of the Church. His lordship is quite a young man, seeing the exalted position he has attained. At Lourdes he was the simplest amongst the pilgrims. Going down to the grotto and kneeling amongst the throng, this pious confessor performed his devotions in a childlike manner. Full of faith, hope, and charity, the good bishop's appearance upon the cold floor of the Virgin's shrine was a source of edification to all who had the happiness to see him.

August 4th.—His lordship, Dr. Moreno, said Mass at nine o'clock, and gave Holy Communion to a large number of persons. Vespers were sung at two o'clock pontifically, and solemn Benediction of the Blessed Sacrament given by the Bishop. His lordship preached after Vespers to a large congregation, as I was informed, for after breakfast I left Lourdes for Pau, a city 24 miles to the south-west of the former town.

My advice to visitors to Lourdes who intend making a lengthened stay there is to take a few short excursions to the many beautiful places situated at convenient distances; for I found that the continual strain upon the senses by the daily and hourly scenes witnessed at the shrine of Our Lady of Lourdes is almost too overpowering to be borne without producing a degree of oppression which it is not well for one leaving the bustle and scramble of worldly existence to be constantly subjected to with safety. For this purpose I went to-day to Pau, passing in going my old friends at St. Pé, and getting a glimpse of the beautiful Calvary of Monte Betharram, of which more anon. What I saw at Pau I must reserve for the next chapter.

CHAPTER IV.

Visit to Pau.—The Château.—Abd-el-Kader.—Queen Isabella.—Beautiful Cemetery.—An English Confessor.—Return to Lourdes.—Solemn and interesting Ceremonials. — Brilliant Illuminations and Processions.—Interview with the Curé Peyramale.

PAU, the ancient capital of Navarre, is one of the most fashionable places of resort in France. It is now the chief town in the department des Basses Pyrénées, situated at an easy distance from Bayonne and the celebrated wateringplaces of Biarritz and St. Jean de Luz, and not too far from the mineral baths of Cauterets Barages and Bagneres-de-Bigorre. During the season there are from ten to twelve thousand visitors residing there, the greater number of whom come from England and America. Pau has many objects which must interest those visiting the place. Its ancient château, built in 1363, is a fine structure, and, since its restoration by Louis Philippe, is kept in good order. The tapestries to be seen in the château are amongst the most choice of any to be found in France ; in themselves they are worth a visit, and are all the more satisfactory in that the subjects are treated in a manner which

A Month at Lourdes.

cannot give any offence to the most fastidious. The room is shown in which Henry IV. was born, and also the tortoise-shell cradle in which he was nursed. A very interesting collection of tables, vases, and statuary, made of beautifully variegated marbles, got from the adjacent quarries of the Pyrenees, is to be seen in the château. These objects are of exquisite workmanship and design. Indeed, the interior of the château may be said to be a combination of marbles not easily to be paralleled. Abd-el-Kader was a resident in the château for a considerable period, and its roof lately gave a shelter to Queen Isabella of Spain. The churches of St. Jacques and St. Martin are very fine erections, and will repay a visit to them. The Palais de Justice, the museum, and library are also not to be passed over without a call. The park and gardens are laid out with consummate taste and wonderful skill for effect. The view of the Pyrenean mountains and valleys from the park is perhaps the most exquisite to be seen in the whole range of scenery which the ever-varying points of observation in those regions present.

I have always made it a point, when visiting

strange places, to look in upon the "City of the Dead," for I hold that a good insight into the character of the people is to be had by seeing the mode in which they bury their dead. Prompted by this feeling, I paid a visit to the cemetery of Pau, and was highly gratified with what I saw therein. In a country where numerous descriptions of marbles abound, it is not surprising that the monuments erected over the graves are of the choicest description. Many bear the names of men who distinguished themselves at the Malakoff, Inkerman, Sevastopol, Castel Fidardo, and Solferino, and some in earlier battles. The neatly tended tombs, upon which the rarest of flowers of sunny France are piously cultivated, give to this City of the Dead the appearance of a richly-stocked flower-garden. Several neatly-constructed oratories, having beautiful altars, are to be found here. The number of ladies and gentlemen and young children whom I saw, with tiny watering-cans sprinkling the flowers and grassy beds, clearly show how affectionately the memory of those who had gone into their houses of eternity are remembered. The depth of affection which influenced such living care must be great on the whole. Pau may well feel proud of its cemetery, and strangers visiting its well laid out grounds might well exclaim:

"Ah! it were pleasant to the grave to go,
If one were sure to be buried so."

During the season horse-racing, fox-hunting, and polo matches are of weekly occurrence. Wolves, too, are put upon their mettle, and bears are made fair game to the sporting ladies and gentlemen who spend their time and money in this pleasant autumn residence. Persons who set a high value upon personal expenses had better not make a long stay in this city. In the church of the Jesuit Fathers, in the Rue de Montpensier, there is generally to be found a confessor who speaks the English language, and whose services are cheerfully given to the English-speaking Catholics who may be visitors at Pau.

Having spent a very agreeable day, we took train for Lourdes, where we arrived in the evening. The railway from Lourdes to Pau runs alongside of the Gave, and scenes of surpassing loveliness are presented to the traveller's view along the route. Great preparations were made to-day at Lourdes in order to worthily celebrate the Feast of the Perpetual Adoration of the Most Blessed Sacrament, the principal festival of the diocese of Tarbes, which was to be observed on the morrow. It need hardly be stated that this feast is highly venerated by the people of the diocese, many of whom, living far off in their mountain fastnesses, came into town in the evening to prepare themselves for obtaining the indulgences of the feast by approaching the tribunal of penance.

August 5th.—To-day was ushered in with a brilliant sun shining refulgently in the heavens. The leafy bowers surrounding the church and grotto shone out in all their various tints of shade, made more beautiful by the refreshing showers of the previous day. The freshly mown hay, as it lay in its swards, distilled its richest perfumes, and the eglantine and honeysuckle lent their choicest odours to add to the offerings which nature presented on this joyous morning. Scarcely had the syren notes of the nightingale died away when the merry lark rose from his dewy bed to carol forth his matutinal hymn at heaven's gate. Even the lively grasshoppers made the earth's green carpet vocal with harmonious chirpings. With early dawn came the stalwart peasantry, accompanied by their female relatives, to

A Month at Lourdes.

Our Lady's church. Nothing could be more picturesque than the appearance of the women. From the close proximity to Spain, many of the women have a tinge of Spanish features, which makes them all the more interesting to look at, in that they are not so darkly shaded as are their sisters of Castile or Andalusia. The dress of these females is calculated to give additional effect to their appearance. A sort of turban, formed by an ingenious manipulation of a silken handkerchief around their heads, has a very neat and tidy look, and shows that even now the fashions of the Moors are not obliterated. The younger portion of the females wear nicely arranged capulets, which, fastened upon their brows, are gracefully thrown over their shoulders, extending down to the waist. As those capulets are of various colours, they have a very pleasing effect when seen amongst a crowd.

Holy Mass commenced at five b'clock, and from that hour until noon each of the twenty-two altars was surrounded by a cordon of priests, all eagerly awaiting their opportunity to offer up the Holy Sacrifice. The white robes of the Dominicans, the brown dress of the Capuchin and Franciscan Fathers, the sombre garb of the

Jesuits, and other coloured habits worn by the clergy, were very interesting. Whilst at the grotto in the morning I witnessed a very touching incident. A young woman, accompanied by her mother and a young girl, came from the town to the grotto. The former woman was dressed in her bridal robes, wearing a wreath of orange blossoms upon her brow. She came to ask the help of Our Blessed Lady to keep her and her intended husband from all the snares of their enemies. She entered the railings which surround the grotto, and made her humble supplications; having done which, she retraced her steps to the parish church, and took her part in the ceremony which was to make her life happy. If the kindly expressed wishes of all who saw and admired her devotion could add to her welfare, that young voyager on the sea of life might feel herself assured of bright days.

High Mass commenced at ten o'clock. The Right Rev. Dr. Moreno pontificated, and five attendant priests assisted. The gorgeous vestments worn by his lordship and the priests were the gift of the Empress Eugénie. At the High Mass a great number received Holy Communion, and indeed at all the Masses during the morning the altar rails were thronged with devout communicants. Immediately after the Bishop had concluded his Mass, the Blessed Sacrament was placed on the summit of the tabernacle, where it remained the whole of the afternoon up to the time for Vespers. The altar presented a strikingly grand effect. Hundreds of wax candles were burning within the sanctuary; the lamps were all lit, and a series of golden vine leaves hung in graceful festoons, which, in their beautiful shadings, as the sun's rays poured through the several stained-glass windows, gave an iris-like appearance to the scene. Pontifical Vespers began at seven p.m., the Bishop again officiating. Just as his lordship entered the church, dressed in his full pontificals, the innumerable candles throughout the lofty nave and the several chapels flashed into flame instantaneously, by means which I have already described. The grand organ sent forth its thrilling tones, and the numerous retinue of clergymen who followed his lordship within the rails of the sanctuary deployed to their places. The rich display of vestments, the streams of light reflected from the many precious gems on and around the altar, the jewelled monstrance in which the Blessed Sacrament was enclosed, the perfumed incense given out by the three crucibles, the noble appearance of the Bishop as he stood upon the platform of the altar holding the monstrance in his hands, and having his white mitre upon his brow, the glittering appearance of the hundreds of flags as the heated atmosphere of the basilique caused them to flutter upon their staffs, and the assemblage of bishops, priests and people, formed a *coup d'œil* which can never fade from the memory of those who were present, and which prompted an American gentleman, who has represented his government in an important position in France for the past fifteen years, to remark to me, "If there is any spot on earth near to heaven, this is it." The singing of the solemn chant composed by St. Gregory was grand and imposing. No one could mistake for a moment the union which existed between the hearts of the singers and the sentiments which they sung. When solemn benediction was over, a procession of several guilds, composed of women and men, with the clergy and bishops following, left the basilique for the grotto, singing hymns and spiritual canticles as they marched along. Each one in

A Month at Lourdes.

the procession carried a lighted candle, and each confraternity or guild bore before it a banner. As the processionists moved down from the church by the zig-zag path along the side of the hill, the lights ever shifting through the trees and shrubs, rendered the scene, viewed from the lower ground, a very effective one. When the procession had reached the grotto, and had filled up the large space around, his lordship, still in his pontifical robes, recited the Litany of Loretto, the vast crowd making the responses. After the Litany, the "Magnificat" was sung by all the assembly. The bishop then returned to the basilique, and the immense concourse of people dispersed to the various parts of the town wherein they were located, carrying their lighted tapers in their hands and singing sacred songs. I should mention that the Rev. Père Ambrose, principal priest of the Carmelite church at Bagneres-de-Bigorre, preached a very able and eloquent sermon on the Blessed Eucharist, and on the glories of the Church Militant, Suffering, and Triumphant.

August 6th.—To-day there were many lingering about the grotto and church, finding it hard to tear themselves away from so precious a spot. Dr. Moreno was early in the church, and celebrated the seven o'clock Mass at the high altar. The Right Rev. Dr. Serra, of Daulia, formerly Vicar Apostolic of Australia, came to-day to Lourdes from Spain. His lordship is a most venerable-looking prelate.

August 7th.—The members of the Benedictine Community of Betharram had a visit to-day from their lordships Drs. Moreno and Serra, both of whom offered up the Holy Sacrifice before leaving for Betharram. As I was anxious to have an introduction to the venerable Monsignor Peyramale, the curé of St. Pierre's church, Lourdes, I called upon him. The venerable curé did not on that occasion show any signs of failing strength beyond what is incidental to a man approaching eighty years of age. I was hoping that his life might be spared to complete the second great work in which he had engaged—the erecting of a new church for the parish of Lourdes, dedicated to St. Peter. But human aspirations and hopes are very insignificant in the decrees of Him in whose hands are life and death. Within a short month after my speaking with Monsignor Peyramale, the cares and anxieties of this world were removed from his thoughts, and the kindly heart which had beaten in his manly bosom was laid in the tomb. Before saying anything more personal to the departed curé, I will say a few words about the undertaking which absorbed his every thought—his church. The old church of St. Pierre at Lourdes stands in a very awkward situation at present. When in the eleventh century the venerable pile was erected, Lourdes, no doubt, was a far different place to what it is now. Surrounded with butchers' shambles, stalls for old and new clothes, and other wares, the nuisance created by the noise of the vendors is very distracting to the congregation worshipping in the church, joined to which, the church blocks up several streets which open on it, and causes some commotion amongst the fiercely contending drivers of vehicles. The municipal authorities agreed to give the curé a sum of £10,000 to enable him to build a new church in a suitable locality. This offer the good curé closed with, and forthwith a large handsome church was designed and put into the hands of the builders. The municipal subsidy was to be given when the church's walls were brought to their intended height. This has been done; but changes having taken place in the rulers of

France, the municipality have harked back in their bargain.

It is needless to say that the great expenses caused by many works at the basilique, &c., have not been favourable to the project of the new church; still, from time to time, the visitors to Lourdes did not forget the noble conduct of the Curé Peyramale when he was fighting the battle of the shrine at the grotto against all the powers of this world; and, believing that some recognition of those services required support in his new labours, have in many instances come to his aid. The projected church, like the basilique, stands over a very noble Crypt church. Although not so large as Nôtre Dame, it is a more massive building. The sanctuary is a very large one, the ceiling of which will be supported by four marble columns, while that of the nave will be sustained by ten columns.

All the columns are now in their positions, and are of the most charming description of the coloured marbles of the Pyrenees, costing a pretty large sum to turn them out in the style in which they are. Each column is formed of one piece; and the height cannot be less than twenty feet. The columns for the clere-

A Month at Lourdes. 77

story and aisles are of the same material, but of course of smaller dimensions. I said that some had remembered the good deeds of the curé. I give the names of those who have charged themselves with the cost of the columns, taking those in the sanctuary first. 1. Diocese of Nantes, 1876. 2. Monsignor Vital, Bishop of Olinda, Brazil. 3 and 4. The National Pilgrims from Paris, 1876. Those in the nave are— 1. Diocese of Beauvoise, 1876. 2. Diocese de Perpignan, 1876. 3. Diocese of Limoges, 1876. 4. Mr. and Mrs. Henry Munster, 1876. 5. M. and Madame Henri Lasserre, Paris, 1876. 6. Madame Blavette, 1876. 7. Alphonse Leblas, Paris, 1876. 8. Pilgrims from Rome, 1876. 9. Monsignor Capel, Catholic University, London, 1876. 10. Belgian Pilgrims, 1876.

A word before leaving this church about two of the donors. Henri Lasserre, who wrote the work "Nôtre Dame de Lourdes," so highly spoken of by His Holiness the Pope, is a gentleman of independent means in the vicinity of Paris, and Henry Munster's fate at a fire in the hotel in America in 1876, will be remembered by all readers of the public papers. Mr. Munster sat for a time for the borough of Cashel. His mother visited Lourdes in 1875, there she received favours at the grotto of Our Lady, and was effectually cured of an illness, which troubled her for many years. A marble tablet in the floor of the grotto recounts the cure of Madame Munster.

Having inspected the church, I and my American friend already alluded to went to pay our respects to the curé. We found him in his parlour, the walls of which were covered with sectional drawings of his new church, and also a full view of it when completed. No one could mistake the curé's desire of seeing the wish of his heart accomplished. Rising up from the midst of his drawings, we stood before a grand specimen of a man of tall and noble features, which clearly showed that the cares of the busy life he had led during the past twenty years had left their impress upon his countenance. He received us most cordially, and entered freely into conversation with us. To any question relative to the apparitions of Our Lady he readily supplied the required information. Those *faithful* (?) guides, Murray and Co., having mentioned in their books that Bernadetta Soubirous had gone insane, and was confined in a lunatic asylum, he smilingly answered that Bernadetta was a professed nun in the convent of the Sisters of Charity at Nevers, close to Lyons. To the further question if Bernadetta was aware of what had been done at the rocks of Massabielle, where she had conversed with Our Lady, the curé answered by saying that ladies who had been at Lourdes from time to time had called to see Sister Mary Bernard (her name in religion), and, as ladies will talk when they meet, Bernadetta was aware of all that occurred at Lourdes. Having ascertained that I was a native of Ireland, the curé brightened up, and spoke in high praise of the Island of Saints, winding up his remarks by declaring that "Ireland was a privileged nation." Asking me to what diocese I belonged, and being told Armagh, he inquired where the bishop resided, and the population of the cathedral city. When I answered him, he seemed astonished that so few inhabitants were therein. I explained that St. Patrick, the Apostle of Ireland, had formed his See at Armagh, and it has retained the primacy to our day. He spoke of the cathedral church. When I informed him that a pile worthy of the faith of Ireland has been raised, which has taken nearly forty years to bring to its present state, he shrugged his shoulders, and said he hoped it would not take him forty years to finish his church. Alas! within less than forty days the good and noble curé passed away to receive the reward of his labours here below, and to leave to other hands to carry to completion the magnificently designed church which his zeal and piety have so far advanced.

CHAPTER V.

Church Psalmody.—Saint Augustine—Great Assemblage of Carmelite Fathers to honour Dr. Moreno.—Market Day.—French and Irish Modes of transacting Business.—Visit to Betharram.

AUGUST 9TH.—On this day a special thanksgiving to God, for the miraculous preservation of his lordship the Right Rev. Dr. Moreno from the hands of his enemies, was given in the basilique. To add to the imposing nature of the day's ceremonies, the Carmelite Fathers from the surrounding convents came to Lourdes. A deputation of forty young men from the military academy at Tarbes, in their bright uniform, also came down. His lordship sang High Mass, and within the sanctuary seats

A Month at Lourdes.

were provided for the military academicians, whose voices were heard with good effect in the musical portion of the Mass. The choir was composed of the Young Men's Society of Bagneres-de-Bigorre, whose proficiency in sacred psalmody has made for them a name throughout the South of France. If any of my readers had the pleasure of hearing the Bernais singers, when they visited these countries, some twenty or more years ago, they will be able to form some idea of the beauty of the chanting which took place in the Church of Nôtre Dame de Lourdes on that remarkable day. The Bernais came from the neighbourhood of Bagneres-de-Bigorre. It is only on an occasion such as this that the beauty and sublimity of Catholic worship can be witnessed and appreciated. Does any one desire to see the Church celebrate her great festivals? If so, let him be present at the Feast of the Assumption. Clothed in magnificent vestments, the celebrant and his attendant clergy stand before the high altar; the Canon of the Mass is being read, the tinkling of the bells announces the great and glorious Act about to take place—the Man-God descending from His Heavenly Throne to reign upon our altars. The divinely appointed minister pronounces the awful words of consecration, he raises the Sacred Host aloft, the congregation reverently bow their heads in humble adoration, their souls are touched with a holy love, and prayers from the deep diapason of the heart ascends like fragrant incense to the Throne of the Almighty Lord of Hosts! The choir sends forth its voice in sacred songs of adoration, praise, and gratitude. It is at such a moment that the strains of a Gregory, Artine, Palestrina, or Mozart become truly religious, not merely by being linked to words expressive of supplication and praise, or the enumeration of the attributes of the Deity, and declaring the homage which devotion pays to Him, but their power is felt as an agency acting upon the soul through the senses. Thus they make the nerves thrill, when they touch, purify, and elevate the mind, and they become over us an absorbing influence by which God communicates with man through the harmonies of nature! What wonder that the great St. Augustine, when visiting the Cathedral of Milan, to hear St. Ambrose preach, and when he was not a member of the true Church, declared, as he entered the Cathedral during Holy Mass, " As the voices of the choir flowed

A Month at Lourdes. 83

in at my ears, truth was instilled into my heart, and the affections of piety overflowed in sweet tears of joy." A very interesting part of to-day's proceedings in the church was the reception of the Sacrament of Confirmation by three young boys, at the hands of the bishop, during an interval of the Mass. The youths knelt within the sanctuary, and received Holy Communion from the bishop. Before Confirmation the boys were taken into the vestry, from which they shortly emerged, each bearing a large wax candle in his hand. The bishop sat upon his throne and had each youth presented to him, and went through the ceremony with all the beautiful impressiveness belonging to the holy ordinance prescribed by the Church. After Confirmation the left arm of each boy was encircled with a white armlet indicative of the determination to fight for the truth of our holy religion. I saw the boys several times during the day, and observed that they still wore their armlets. Pontifical Vespers were given at two p.m., the same choir giving their services. The fervour of the crowds, who thronged the church from early morn until it was closed at night, must have consoled the heroic Confessor for whose safe deliverance many of them had come from a considerable distance to thank the Almighty Creator of the universe for His protection of the good prelate.

Lourdes is favoured with a market on each alternate Thursday; I availed myself of the opportunity of seeing how the farmers and cattle dealers conducted their business. As early as four o'clock the air was filled with the pleasant tinkling of the string of bells which each cow or other animal employed in drawing waggons or coaches had around its neck. Here I may remark that the cows are a hardly-dealt-with animal in Southern France. It is not enough that they have to give milk; but they are likewise compelled to draw the carts, plough and harrow the land, and do all such work as is only performed by horses in these countries. Nothing can exceed the kindness with which the French people treat their dumb animals, never striking them, but rather inducing them to put forth their strength by acts of kind treatment. The cows have veils upon their faces, and their bodies are covered by neatly made crochet-work coverlets. These coverings are intended as a protection against the musquitoes, so numerous in the country.

Having gone into the town where the principal part of the fair or market was held, it took some time ere I could believe that I was not in Ireland. The noise and bustle betwixt buyers and sellers was something to be remembered. Here was a man driving a bargain with a woman, the owner of four or five pigs, and to one not acquainted with the scenes to be seen amongst similar persons in an Irish fair, the idea that would suggest itself to his mind would be that physical violence was contemplated. The immemorial " penny," or rather the " ten centime " of the day, was brought into requisition, accompanied with the usual moisture, to clench the bargain. It was really a good chance of viewing the French peasantry in their natural state of vivaciousness. Here were also the small farmers, some having a bushel of wheat, others a like quantity of rye, maize, or barley, all turning their little stock of produce into cash. Bunches of flax, linen and woollen yarns, fruit and vegetables—in fact, everything which the land produces, or the patient industry of the people could bring forth—were here for sale. It would be doing these simple-minded people an injustice if I omitted to state the fact that, amidst all the excitement, not one was to be seen under the influence of intoxicating spirits. Indeed, so far as that goes, I can safely aver that in my travels in France, covering nearly 2,000 miles, and occupying the better part of a month, I did not see a single person under the influence of strong drink.

August 10th.—Many strangers arrived and visited the church and grotto, all of whom, upon leaving, bore away with them vessels containing water from the miraculous fountain. Amongst those who appeared to-day was a veritable Palmer, dressed in all the characteristics of the pious traveller one reads of in Froissart. His scrip and staff, his venerable beard, large prayer-book, beads and crosses, truly proclaimed the devotee, whilst his sunburnt countenance clearly showed that he had traversed many lands in the pursuit of his pilgrimages to the shrines made remarkable by their sanctity. His was not the piety which trafficked in its manifestation, for I saw him refuse coins which were proffered to him.

August 11th.—To day, after breakfast, I left Lourdes for the purpose of visiting the Church of Nôtre Dame and the Calvary at Montaut-Betharram, and was richly repaid for my journey. Visitors to Lourdes must not upon any account forego a visit to Betharram, because if they do so, half the gratification which they otherwise would receive will be lost to them; and as Betharram is only fifteen miles from Lourdes, it will not greatly encroach upon their time to run over to that most interesting locality.

Betharram is amongst the most ancient and renowned shrines of Our Lady in France, and therefore some account of its origin will prove interesting to my Catholic readers. The following sketch, which for the sake of space I have considerably abridged, is taken from the history of the Venerable Pierre Marca, who was a priest at Betharram, and who took part in the ceremonies of the founding of the Calvary by the Archbishop of Auch in 1616. Tradition says that a church was founded here towards the close of the 10th century, having its origin in the finding of a miraculous statue of the Blessed Virgin. It is recorded that a young peasant girl, who was gathering flowers on the bank of the Gave, opposite Betharram, overbalanced herself and fell into the stream. Finding herself sinking, she implored the protection of the Mother of God, who then appeared to her, and plucking a branch of a white rose tree, threw it into the flood. The girl grasped it, and came safely to land. It is a most singular fact, and highly corroborative of the miraculous escape of the pious peasant girl, that on the rock where she saw the Virgin stand, a fountain gushed forth, which to this day sends its waters into the Gave. This fountain's source, although adjoining the Gave, is on an elevation above the river's flood. The rescued girl and her friends presented to the church of Our Lady at Estelle—close to the present Betharram—a golden branch. Thus we have the name of Beau-Rameau, or Fine-Branch, or, as it is now called, "De Betharram," in the Gascon tongue.

One of the Fathers of Betharram, who has recently published a short history of the sacred place, which was issued with the imprimatur of Mgr. Lacroix, Bishop of Bayonne, in alluding to the story of the girl and the rose branch, says, "Betharram deserves still more the title of 'Fine-Branch,' in comparison to that which in the books of the Saints is compared to the cedar of Lebanon, to the cypress of Sion, to the palms of Cadres, to the rose-trees of Jericho, to the olives of the plains. Here it was that Mary established her dwelling-place in the midst of nature in all its beauty, in one of the delightful valleys of the Pyrenees, and blessed with the most charming climate in the world. Most of the trees are emblems of, and symbolize with perfection the graces of the treasury which God has placed under their graceful shade, and they interlace and mingle their branches in a dome of verdure above His Holy Sanctuary." In the month of September, 1616, five villagers of Montauth, situated opposite Betharram, were enjoying their noontide refection, sitting on the slope of the river's bank. The sky was clear and bright, the air calm and still, and the distant horizon gave no sign of an approaching storm. All at once the villagers hear a sound of a tempest in the direction of Betharram. They saw the Cross, which the Archbishop of Auch (Blessed Leonard de Trappes) had some time before placed on the summit of the mountain, which dominates the church of Betharram, fall to the ground, struck down by the blast. But soon the whirlwind ceased, and the cross again reared itself. A dazzling light, of splendid brilliancy, crowns the cross; so bright and dazzling that the five villagers were scarcely able to gaze upon it. They run, and as it were, fly forward with high beating hearts, and they approach nearer and nearer to the miraculous appearance. When they have had their fill of joy, they hasten to communicate what has happened to the faithful of the neighbourhood.

This miracle caused a great sensation at Béarn. The Sectaries dared not doubt of its having happened. The neighbouring populations were so convinced of its truth that they hastened to testify their joy by processions, in which they took part, for days afterwards, to the spot where it occurred. Five years later the Bishop of Auch instituted an inquiry by his delegates. They were joined by the authorities of Estelle, who were solemnly sworn to testify to the truth, and subjected to those severe rules which the Church always enforces to verify miracles, and this inquiry conclusively established the truthfulness of the occurrence.

St. Roch.—This holy Father of the church, who is patron saint of Betharram, was, I believe, an Irishman. Certain it is that Betharram, highly favoured place as it is,

A Month at Lourdes.

has not the exclusive claim of being under the patronage of St. Roch. At Bingen, midway on the Rhine, there is a favourite temple dedicated to St. Roch. No one that has visited the charming scenery, of which Bingen forms so central a point for viewing, can forget the church of St. Roch, or, as it is there called, "Rochuscappelle," on the east brow of Rochusberg. This chapel, standing 341 feet above the Rhine, presents one of the finest views among many which are to be seen along that classic river.

At Betharram there were so many well-attested miracles, that Rome could not long remain in ignorance of the fact. Accordingly we find that a Commission was appointed to investigate into the truth of the reports reaching the Holy Father. Popes Urban VIII., Alexander VII., Gregory XVI., and Pius IX. (all of happy memory), have all borne testimony to the truth of the miracles wrought at the Church and Calvary of Betharram, and by special briefs have conferred many indulgences on those who piously visit the sacred locality. Emperors, kings, and princes did not think it unworthy of their care to enrich with costly ornaments and rich foundations the shrine of Our Lady. Henry IV., Louis XIII., Louis XIV., Napoleon III., Marie Antoinette, the Duchesses d'Angoulême, De Chambord, De Montaigu, the Empress Eugenie, and many of the great ones of the earth, have paid willing homage at the shrine of Our Lady at Betharram. Perhaps one of the most illustrious visitors to Betharram was the sainted Archbishop of Auch, the blessed Leonard de Trappes, who, in 1616, saw upon the mountain over Betharram, a miraculous appearance of the Holy Cross, and conceived the idea of forming on the mountain a *via crucis*. This is a wonder to all who behold its soul-inspiring monuments, whose hearts must be rent with grief whilst contemplating the tableaux of the doleful journey by which man's salvation was accomplished.

During one of those evil periods when the world is seemingly given over to the wickedness of man, Betharram fell a prey to the fury of the Huguenots, who despoiled its sanctuaries, desecrated its Calvary, and massacred the pious men and women whose hitherto peaceful convents gave them a home. No sooner had France purged herself of the leprosy, than haste was made to restore the damage done by the

A Month at Lourdes.

fiendishly urged Vandals, and in a short time the church, convents, seminaries, and Calvary of Betharram once more assumed their former appearance, and stand to-day attesting the impotency of man's rage when confronted with the breath of an angry God. When attending the Vatican Council Monsignor La Croix, Bishop of Bayonne, in whose diocese Betharram is situated, solicited and obtained from the Sovereign Pontiff a grant of a plenary indulgence to all those who, complying with the requisite conditions, perform the Way of the Cross and visit the church of the Fathers of the Sacred Heart of Jesus. Having said this much about the origin of Betharram, I ought to say a few words on the locality itself, previous to asking my readers to ascend with me the mountain's side upon which the Calvary and its many beautiful churches, fourteen in all, are situated. The church of Nôtre Dame stands upon the left bank of the Gave, and, as seen from the railway station, about half a mile off, one has but a faint idea of its grand proportions and richly emblazoned interior. The Gave here makes a sharp curve around a spur of the Pyrenees, and as its waters during their long course receive considerable accessions from the many tributary streams which flow into it, its volume at Betharram is very considerable. A bridge spans the river close to the church, the battlements of which are gracefully festooned with a peculiar description of ivy, growing down in garlands until the branches touch the stream beneath. Immediately alongside of the bridge is a large conventual establishment for ladies, and further on, nearer to the church, is the seminary and monastery of the above-named Fathers. Nôtre Dame is built in the massive style so peculiar to the Gascon churches, which, in their proximity to Spain, have borrowed a good share of the architecture of that country. The numerous chapels within the church are made resplendent by the noble votive gifts of the several donors, some of whom I have already named above. The paintings of the "Way of the Cross" are really grand, whilst the many frescoes, with their interesting subjects, are highly devotional to look upon. Immediately in front of the church there is a statue of St. Roch, the patron saint of the district, standing under a canopy, the whole surmounting a well from which a copious flow of water is continuously poured into a basin. The village of

A Month at Lourdes. 95

Betharram stands about half a mile further down the banks of the Gave, where accommodation can be had by persons paying a visit to this place. If visitors object to put up with the fare obtainable at Betharram village, the distance from Pau is only nine miles, and ready access thereto can be had either by rail or coach for a few francs. Apart from religious attractions, Betharram deserves a visit. Situated in the midst of the valley of the Pyrenean range through which the impetuous Gave wends its way, the disciples of Isaac Walton need not lack plentiful occupation in the gentle art, no man's leave being required; whilst those more adventurously inclined will find food enough for any amount of powder they may carry in their pouches. The peasantry are most civil, and willing to oblige, and the stranger who can control his temper, and curb his impatience because people do not at once comprehend all he wishes them to do, will get along pretty well in his travels. It is time I should now return to the calvary at Betharram; but as it is too important to treat of at the end of a chapter, I must reserve my remarks upon the illustrious spot.

To all who take an interest in the church

and grotto of Our Lady of Lourdes, and who remember the heroic conduct of the lately deceased Curé Peyramale, a perusal of the following touching letter of the once shepherdess Bernadette Soubirous received since my return from Lourdes, and for which I am indebted to a kind friend in France, will doubtless afford pleasure.

Nevers, 15th Sept., 1877.

DEAR FRIEND,—I very much regret not having been able to write to you sooner; but the so sudden death of our dear and venerable Curé, has quite upset me. What a cruel loss to the dwellers at Lourdes! They would indeed be ungrateful if they did not perceive in the death of our dear and good pastor an excess of zeal of the glory of God and the salvation of souls! It seems that the grief he experienced on account of the new church had much to do with hastening his death. I am by no means astonished; he had so much at heart the work he had inaugurated so well. We must bow to the designs of God, without whose Will nothing is done. It was on the feast of the Nativity of the very Holy Virgin that this crushing news reached me. At nine o'clock my dear sister Nathalie came to seek me at the tribune, and told me that a despatch had arrived the previous evening to say that the curé was most dangerously ill. Then came another the same evening, which announced his death! To tell you what I have suffered would be impossible. But just so much as the pain I have suffered has been great, equally sweet has been the consolation I have experienced on reading that our lamented curé had the happiness of receiving the Holy Sacrament with his mind unclouded; and that he was comforted in his last moments by the Abbé Pomian, the friend of his heart, his faithful and zealous assistant.

The very Holy Virgin came to seek our good Father on the day of her Nativity, to repay the sacrifices and severe trials he willingly suffered owing to his love for her! The only consolation we have is, that we have another protector more in heaven, and this may assuage our pain.

In praying you to be so kind as to remember me in a small part of your prayers, I offer you my most respectful compliments, and have the honour to be, &c.,

SISTER MARIE BERNARD SOUBIROUS.

This letter is not like the writing of a maniac, as some English authors, who have written of the apparitions of Our Lady at Lourdes, would fain make their readers believe.

CHAPTER VI.

Betharram.—The Calvary.—Wonderful Sculptures.—The Crucifixion.—The Impenitent Thief.—Mary Magdalene.—The Pie Mater.—Return to Lourdes.—The Festival of the Assumption.—Great Processions and Illuminations.

A SHORT distance from the principal entrance to the Church of Nôtre Dame, the first Station of the Calvary is placed. As the fourteen chapels, in which are placed the Stations, nearly resemble each other, with one or two exceptions, I may here describe these sacred edifices. The chapels are built of cut-stone; the altars are of marble, and over each altar is inserted a sacred relic. The carving of the doorways is very chaste in design and execution. The Way of the Calvary being zigzag, the chapels are so placed that the light is thrown upon the representations of the several stages of Our Lord's dolorous journey, which are fixed above the altar. This intromission of light has a very happy effect upon the figures and paintings with which the chapels are filled. All the figures are carved in Caen stone, and exceed life-size, standing out distinct from the walls of the chapels. Each chapel is enclosed with handsome bronze railings, having entrance gates in the centre to admit the clergy and people when performing the "Way of the Cross." I may add that the mountain, from its base to its summit, is clothed in a thick wood of acacias, walnuts, firs, and oak trees, whose lofty height show them to have been planted long ago, and whose rich foliage gives a sombreness to the path by which the people ascend. The first Station shows Our Lord in the garden of Olives; His chosen disciples asleep whilst their Lord was praying. The second pourtrays the treason of Judas; third, Jesus before Caiphas; the fourth, the scourging at the pillar. The fiendish fury of the Jews, whose knotted cords tore and lacerated the divine flesh of the Saviour, has been well brought out in the demoniacal looks which the sculptor has given to their countenances. The fifth Station, where Christ is being crowned with thorns, is a most striking representation of that cruel operation.

The church in which this Station is placed was the gift of King Louis XIII. It is a kingly erection. The building is surmounted by three cupolas of exquisite design, of beautiful white marble. And there are three altars in it, which are quite in keeping with its style of architecture. Over the entrance is a tablet, which bears the following inscription: "LA CHAPELLE DE ST. LOUIS. DOIT SON ERECTION. A LA PIÉTÉ DE LOUIS XIII. SURNOMMÉ LE JUSTE. ELLE FUT DISASTIR PAR LE VANDALISME REVOLUTIONNAIRE EN 1793." In front of the high altar is inscribed: "Mais La Religion Est Immortelle!" This church presents a striking feature of the Calvary to all passengers who travel past Betharram by the railway from Pau to Tarbes. The sixth Station brings before you Our Saviour when presented to the gaze of the rabble by Pilate. I have looked with feelings of intense pain upon the many paintings of the "Ecce Homo" in the great museum of Antwerp, and have seen similar attempts to realise the subject upon canvas by the many inspired geniuses whose works adorn the cathedrals of Cologne, Mayence, Brussels, &c., but to put upon paper my feelings, on beholding the full-sized figure of the Redeemer, as shown in the chapel of the sixth Station of the Cross at Betharram, is beyond my power. To see the flesh, scarified with scourges, livid, and pouring forth blood from every vein and artery; the very bones laid bare, the streams of blood coursing down the blessed face from every thorn so fiercely pressed into the head, the look of commiseration for His cruel torturers amidst all His own afflictions, is enough to bring tears to the eyes of every Christian beholder. This representation of the shameless exposure of the Saviour by the infamous Jews, once seen, can never be obliterated from memory, and makes the soul shudder at the enormity of human wickedness which could so treat the Son of God. At the eighth Station, where our Saviour meets His Blessed Mother, the group which displays this sad encounter, is wonderfully impressive, as is also the ninth, where Our Lord benignantly consoles the daughters of Jerusalem whom He saw weeping over His afflictions. The cruel conduct of the executioners, shown at the tenth Station, who, in their malice, are striving to increase the tortures of the Son of God by drawing His hands and feet to the holes into which the nails were afterwards driven, is brought vividly before you. After passing the tenth Station we arrive at the summit of the Calvary, and find ourselves standing upon a plateau some two acres in extent, around which are grouped the next four stages of the Passion and the Resurrection, with some beautifully executed groups of statuary in keeping with the solemn scene around. Visitors upon entering this plain, on the lofty summit of the hill of Betharram, some 4000 feet above the level of the sea, are struck with wonder at viewing the sublimity of the surrounding scenery. As far as the eye can reach on one side are the lofty peaks of the Pyrenees, whose glacier capped summits are seen far above the clouds, rising up from the valleys below. Looking in another direction, the broad expanse of the waters of the Atlantic as they dash against the coasts of Spain and France are visible. The cities and towns which are placed within a circle of sixty miles around, look as mere specks in the panorama of woods, mountains, lakes, and rivers, presented to the gaze of the onlooker. To repeat the language of a writer already referred to in describing Betharram: " Here Mary has established her dwelling-place in the midst of nature in all its beauty,

A Month at Lourdes. 103

in one of the most delightful valleys of the Pyrenees, and blessed with the most charming climate in the world. Most of the trees here are emblems of, and symbolize with perfection, the graces of the treasury which God has placed under her grateful shade ; and they interlace and mingle their branches lovingly in a vast dome of natural verdure above His holy sanctuary." But it is not with the beauties which bountiful nature spreads around us that I have now to deal. I have to speak of the scenes upon this spot as typified in stone, of the crowning act, by which all human hopes were revived in the beatific hereafter, by the death of the Redeemer of fallen mankind. As you enter the circle, and look towards the south-west, the Crucifixion on the " Hill of Calvary " stands before you. The three crosses are at least twenty feet high, and the figures are considerably above life-size. On the right hand side of the Saviour, the Penitent Thief is suspended upon his cross. His head is humbly cast down upon his breast, with face slightly turned towards Our Saviour. The first finger of the dexter hand is pointed heavenwards ; whilst the Saviour, in His dying agonies, sweetly inclines His head towards the humble penitent, and consolingly points His Divine finger upwards, assuring the dying thief that ere another sun shall have risen, he shall be with Him in Paradise. On the left hand hangs the Impenitent thief, his countenance distorted with rage, his body writhing with agony, his right hand clenched with fiendish anger, as he in his blind fury taunts the Son of God for not releasing him from the ignominious gibbet upon which, for his malefactions, he hangs suspended. The countenance of the wretch clearly shows, as far as the sculptor can, the enormity of the wickedness of the sinner. Standing out against the clear blue sky, the group of the Crucifixion on the Calvary at Betharram, will well repay any trouble or expense incurred by such as feel moved to pay this highly interesting spot a visit. The taking down from the cross, the Entombment, and the Resurrection, have each their respective chapels, and are equally grand in their representations. The latter chapel has three altars—over the centre one is a magnificent painting of the Resurrection, and over each of the others are paintings which must have cost a considerable sum of money to purchase. On the south side of the plateau there is a group of white marble, a

Pieta, the work of the elder Dumoulet of Toulouse, the expense of which was borne by the Marquis Armand-Mathieu d'Angosse and his wife. This group shows the Blessed Virgin with the dead body of her Divine Son lying in her lap, and the expression on the countenance of the afflicted Mother of God might well challenge the compassion of all beholders. On the opposite side of the square, facing the *Pie Mater*, is a statue of Mary Magdalene cast in metal, which finely pourtrays the intensity of the feelings of grief by which the sainted Magdalene was filled on Calvary. The cost of placing those beautiful groups on the lofty plateau must have been considerable. The Chapel of the Resurrection has been specially indulgenced by the Pope. Immediately behind the Calvary is a neatly kept cemetery, in which are interred the remains of the deceased members of the religious communities, who have died at the convents at Betharram. Having thus given a very bald description of the Calvary at Betharram, and the other religious institutions there, I must once more return to Lourdes.

August 12th, 13th, and 14th.—No particular pilgrimages had arrived at Lourdes, but the church and grotto have their crowded votaries from early morn until late at night. On Tuesday afternoon, a large number of people came to Lourdes to assist at the ceremonies of the following day—the "Feast of the Assumption of Our Lady into Heaven." It need not be told to any one who has visited France how deeply the Blessed Virgin is held in esteem by the people. Statues in the public thoroughfares, on the tops of the loftiest mountains, pictures in the houses—the almost universal name of "Marie," borne by the men and women, all incontestably prove the love which the people have. Hence of all the festivals by which the Church honours the Mother of God, none is more attractive to the people than is the festival of the Assumption. No wonder then that so many are seen wending their way to the grotto of the Immaculate Virgin to ask her intercession on the spot where she so recently manifested herself to the little shepherdess, Bernadette Soubirous. A great number of visitors came from Paris, Lyons, Pau, Toulouse, besides many who were staying for the benefit of the mineral waters at Bareges, Cauterets, Bagneres de Bigorre, St. Savure, &c. No wonder that Lourdes on Tuesday evening presented a busy and stirring appearance. The hotels were crowded. The missionaries in charge of the basilique, were busily engaged in preparing the church for the festival, while the numerous clergymen, who came in with their parishioners, were engaged in the confessionals up to a late hour at night, and again from an early hour in the morning. Indeed many remained the whole of the night before the shrine of Our Lady engaged in their pious meditations. At an early hour the people were astir, getting themselves and their houses in order for the day. To say that tens of thousands paid their loving devotions to God at the church and grotto of Our Lady is literally true, and those who came from a distance to witness the ceremonies, must have been well repaid. The numerous altars were constantly and continuously occupied with priests offering up the Holy Sacrifice of the Mass, and thousands of devout communicants surrounded the sanctuary rails to receive the Bread of Life. High Mass over, the crowds went into town to partake of food so as to be present at the Vespers at two p.m., and then to be witnesses of the interesting proceedings which took place at four o'clock. When Vespers were over, the seats were removed from the nave of the basilique, to enable the people who took part in the procession from the town to find accommodation in the church, it being entirely reserved for them. At four p.m., sounds of military music came up from the town, and shortly afterwards were to be seen splendid silken banners, whose richly ornamented folds were fluttering in the sun's rays. The procession was led by three cross-bearers, who walked in the centre of the street, whilst, on either footway, a line of young girls were dressed in white, with blue scarfs around their shoulders, wearing crowns of beautiful flowers upon their innocent heads. As each guild came along, the flag of the sodality was borne aloft. As with the girls and women, so with the men, flags and bannerets were carried in front of each guild. The excellent peal of bells of the basilique poured forth their welcome notes to the people who were wending their way to the church. The procession was accompanied by the municipal guard, whose bright uniforms lent additional variety to the scene. When the clergy of the parish church of St. Pierre were nearing the bridge

A Month at Lourdes.

which spans the Gave, dividing Lourdes proper from the basilique, the superior of the basilique and three other priests, all clothed in costly vestments, and preceded by about twenty boys, suitably attired, left the church and proceeded to the bridge, where the parochial clergy met them, and after some salutations, they both returned to the basilique. Standing on an eminence over the church, and looking down upon the processionists as they came up the incline, the sight was grandly impressive. The bright dresses of the ladies as they marched along the footpaths, and the numerous flag-bearers walking in the centre of the street, looked like a flower-garden whose walks were fringed with violets and roses. The men, too, in their neat and clean attire, formed no small part in the scene, whilst some Eastern Christians, by their picturesque dress, formed a conspicuous object in the grand procession. The Litany of Our Lady of Lourdes was sung by the people, and to hear the sound of some thousand voices chanting the attributes of the Mother of God, as it floated up the side of the mountain, was really grand and inspiring. After solemn Benediction, the processionists left the church and traversed the zigzag way on the side of the hill on which the church stands, to the grotto, where the Litany was again sung, and some prayers recited, after which the parishioners of Lourdes returned to St. Pierre, where they dispersed to re-assemble again at seven p.m. at the basilique. In the meantime the brothers, who attend at the basilique, were not idle. The lofty doorway of the church was surrounded with four bands of coloured globes, and the façade of the church also had a plentiful supply of similar globes placed upon it, whilst around the base, for its whole extent, a cordon of lamps was affixed. The statue of the Virgin which stands in the meadows betwixt the church and Lourdes was decked out in evergreens, and a large circular flower plot surrounding the statue had globes placed amongst its flowers and shrubs, the pedestal of the statue being likewise supplied with lamps. When the ceremonies began at eight o'clock the interior of the building was lit up in the manner described in a former chapter, and need not here be repeated. When the congregation came out of the church, the shades of night tried to descend, but were baffled by the brilliancy which shone from the thousand lamps burning around, upon the church, and upon the statue. A procession was now formed, which wended its way from the church to the grotto, each person bearing a lighted flambeau in his hand, the whole solemnly chanting the "Ave Maria." These were received by the thousands who could not gain admission to the church, and who were assembled around the grotto, with a joyousness too profound to find expression in language, but which their hearts felt, as their moistened eyes clearly showed. When the procession had reached the grotto, the convents of the Carmelites and the Benedictine nuns, on the opposite bank of the Gave, flashed instantaneously into sheets of light. The scene at this moment was the grandest imaginable. The basilique, standing two hundred feet above the crowds, encircled with robes of light of many colours; the shrine of Our Lady, before it thousands of candles burning; convents across the river reflecting back the intense light, and the flowing waters of the Gave turned into a sheet of silver by the contending beams, the statue in the distance like a pillar of light amongst the trees which surround it, the six thousand persons holding lighted flambeaux in their hands, the joy-bells sending forth their mellow peals, the melody of the thousand voices of priests and people all went to form a scene, which any one who had the privilege of witnessing, can never forget. When the devotions at the grotto were concluded, the entire people once more fell into a procession, and proceeded to the statue of Our Lady, around which they grouped themselves. There, after a short prayer, the "Magnificat" was sung by the vast multitude. This being concluded, the procession returned to Lourdes, the people still carrying the lights in their hands, and singing the Litany, whilst several of the houses were illuminated. After again singing the "Magnificat," in the Grand Square of Lourdes, the people dispersed to their respective homes. Any comments upon the sublime devotion I this day witnessed would not do justice to the way in which was observed this glorious festival.

CHAPTER VII.

Argelles. — Peasant Proprietors—St. Luz. — Curious Church.—Wonderful Scenery.—Bareges.—Mineral Waters.—The Pass of the Tourmalet.—Shepherds about to shear the Sheep.—The Valley of the Campan.—Gripp.—Bagneres de Bigorre.—Death of an Actress. — Burial Rites. — The Great Marble Works of M. Gerezut.

AUGUST 16TH.—After the exciting scenes witnessed yesterday a little recreation was found necessary, and accordingly a party of eight was arranged for the purpose of crossing the Pyrenees to visit the mineral baths, &c., at Bagneres de Bigorre. Some idea of the difficulty attending this journey may be formed when I mention that although Bagneres de Bigorre is only fourteen miles, as the crow flies, from Lourdes, it took us the better part of two days to reach the former place, although each carriage was drawn by four spirited horses. Imitating Napoleon I. who made a road across the Alps, his nephew, Napoleon III., constructed a road from Pau across the Pyrenees which displays wonderful engineering skill in its construction. Had Napoleon III. been allowed to remain at the head of affairs in France, he would have completed the road into Spain, for only eighteen miles had to be made at the fall of his dynasty. His memory will never fade away from this part of France as long as the highway made under his auspices endures. Having taken leave of Lourdes, we drove along the valley of the Lavedan affording a pleasing contrast to the bare hills which divide it from Lourdes, passing an old tower, once the property of the Black Prince, whose head-quarters it was during some of the most stirring events of that heroic Prince's war. The splendid crops abounding in this valley show how well the people, who reside upon, and also *own* the land, are versed in the science of practical agriculture. The town of Argelès lies in this beautiful valley, and, from its well-sheltered situation, is said to be the best place for invalids to spend the winter season in. Its population does not exceed two thousand, but the neatness of the dwellings, added to the comfortable appearance of the people, clearly demonstrate the advantages accruing from a peasant proprietary who till their own land, and are thus able to enjoy the full benefits of the fruits of their industry. At the head of the valley stands the town of Pierrefitte, as you approach which, you imagine that

A Month at Lourdes. 115

the hills surrounding it will put a stop to further progress in that direction. The railway from Bayonne ends here, as the mountains are too steep to carry it any further towards Spain. Some of the hills rear their snow-capped summits 7,030 feet above the level of the sea. Whilst allowing the horses some time to bait, a few of us strolled up to the mouth of the gorge, through which the waters of the Gave rolled along at a considerable distance beneath, the lofty trees which line both sides of it, mingling their branches, giving to the scene a grand appearance, which will well repay all who make this journey. The valleys of Cauterets and Luz divide here, the former to the right and the latter to the left. As we were bound by the one taking the left, we drove along for a few hours amidst some of the wildest scenery imaginable. Mountains whose riven sides seemed ready to topple down as you wend your way close at their base, and, anon, the forests of wood which grow along their sides call up encounters with the wolves and bears abounding in their fastnesses which were anything but pleasant to the timid-minded. The village of Luz is situated in the valley we are traversing. There is a peculiarly con-

S—2

structed church in this place. The building formerly was a citadel, but the crusaders turned it into a place of worship.* The church is of the eleventh century and is entered by a machicolated gateway. Battlements surround the exterior of the sacred edifice, provided with loopholes, etc., which clearly show how fiercely the faith was defended by those semi-warriors and clerics—the Templars. A gateway in the southern wall still exists, through which the Catechumens had to pass when leaving the church during those portions of the Mass from which they were excluded. At the entrance of this church is placed upon a pedestal a stone coffin, in which are the remains of a child who died before being baptised. Seven or eight hundred years have rolled by since the child died, and yet is visible the skeleton of the infant lying in its stony bed. The lid of the coffin is slightly raised so as to afford a view of the remains. On a hill commanding the town a handsome new church has been erected by the Empress Eugenie, and dedicated to St. Peter of Solferino. Proceeding from Luz to St. Sauveur the carriage road is in some

* This church was quite in keeping with the character of its founders—half church, half fortress.

of its parts fearful to contemplate. Now scooped out of projection of a rock, and anon poised in mid-air over a rushing torrent, it winds its circuitous way along the right bank of the Gave until it crosses that river by a bridge of a single arch. This bridge is a grand triumph of science. To see it in its lofty position, 216 feet above the stream, you would fancy that it had been a circle which broke in the heavens, the half of which, descending to earth, caught the rocks on either side of the river and bridged its banks. There is an obelisk commemorating the completion of the bridge, and bearing an inscription complimentary to Napoleon III. and his Empress. Few, indeed, are the spots which impress so forcibly the mind of the beholder as does this locality in which nature and art are so commingled, for each lends and borrows charms from the other. The foundation stone of the bridge was laid in 1860, and its erection cost 300,000 francs.

Luz is the seat of the manufacture of the celebrated Crêpe de Bareges, and as we had some ladies of the party, of course their inquisitiveness prompted a visit to some of the weavers' workshops in which the article was being manufactured. The Jacquard looms are very neatly arranged, and the workmen were most obliging. Having refreshed our horses we started for Bareges, where we arrived about seven p.m. This town is situated on the side of a hill, and consists of but one street in which are some really fine hotels. The thermal springs here are famed for their curative qualities. So highly prized are the waters that the Government have erected baths, to which they send invalid soldiers, and hence the semi-military appearance of the crowds you meet in the place. The public baths are really handsome buildings, but, from my idea, having tasted the waters as they came out of the rock, I should be really at death's door before I could be brought to drink of them. The baths are open day and night, are scrupulously clean, and the charges moderate. There are assistants who call at the hotels when desired, and who convey ladies and gentlemen in handsome sedan chairs to the baths. As those using this mode of conveyance need not make their morning toilets previous to bathing, much trouble and annoyance in dressing and undressing is thereby avoided, for the chairs are fully curtained, and

A Month at Lourdes.

the greatest privacy thus preserved. Although Bareges stands nearly 5,000 feet above the sea level, its climate is not so variable as one might expect, for the neighbouring hills afford shelter from the fierce storms which are sometimes experienced amongst the gorges of the Pyrénées. Tourists are fond of staying at Bareges, as it is the centre of a wide range of the bold and romantic scenery which there abounds. Mountains of great height are in view, and are of comparatively easy ascent. The Pic-du-Midi Bigorre looks down from its dominant position, 9,000 feet above the sea level, whilst its lesser raised neighbours are of respectable altitude. The only thing which gave me annoyance during my visit was the miserable hovel in which Catholic worship is carried out. When assisting at Mass you could not help imagining yourself in some mountain chapel of 100 years ago in Ireland. Why such a structure should be allowed to exist in a place frequented by so many wealthy travellers is a wonder to me. There is a convent chapel close to the public baths, which is a simple structure, but very neatly kept. The avalanches of the winter play sad havoc occasionally with Bareges, and whether its churches are sometimes their victims I cannot say, but certainly it would be all the more honourable to the inhabitants if some efforts were made to provide more suitable and becoming sanctuaries for Divine worship.

Those of my readers who have had the gratification of seeing the sun rise amidst mountains, can appreciate my feelings, when early on the morning of the day after our arrival at Bareges I arose, and, accompanied by one of my fellow voyagers, left the hotel before sunrise and ascended for a considerable distance one of the mountains. The valley beneath us was like a sea of molten silver, the fleecy clouds covered fields, houses, and forests, stretching along the bases of the hills. The sky piercing summits of the surrounding Pics, looked like so many rocky points rising up in the midst of the sea. Long before the sun made himself visible to us, the distant mountain tops had caught his rays, and their burnished heads looked like golden pinnacles placed around the shores of the cloud-lake atmosphere in which their bases were enveloped. The glistening of the icy covering of some of the peaks, as Sol's rays fell upon their glacier mantles, gave to the scene

A Month at Lourdes.

a charming appearance which no one could forget, who had once looked upon the works of God as seen in this most grandly arranged scenery.

Having breakfasted, we took the road for Bagneres de Bigorre, some twenty-five miles off across the mountains. Driving along the valley for some hours, we encountered some of the most interesting sights to be found amongst the Pyrenean range. As our road had been a very circuitous one, each turn we made opened up to view a new vista : mountains whose sides from the top to the base, were clothed in woods of various descriptions of tree and shrub, and valleys, as far as the eye could penetrate, filled with large boulders wrenched from their native beds by some of the fierce freaks of nature, and then hurled down the rugged sides of the mountains. There, apparently turned by friction into balls, they lay upon the plains below like a shower of marbles. The wonderful pertinacity displayed by the simple but industrious peasantry, who, here but sparsely placed, is truly admirable. A patch of land, hardly a rood in extent, perched upon the side of the mountain, is seized upon and made productive. The only wonder is how on earth human beings could ascend and descend to such airy situations. Another interesting feature is the numerous flocks of sheep, whose woolly coats give them the appearance of so many mushrooms as they browse in their inaccessible pastures. Their quiet is seldom disturbed except by the eagle or the isard. Such are some of the scenes the traveller beholds as he journeys through this grand valley towards the pass of the Tourmalet, by which he crosses the Pyrenees on his way to Bigorre. But before he doubles the pass I would advise him to halt for a moment and turn his face along the valley through which he had been travelling, and take in, if he can, the grandeur of the scene which nature presents to his view. Standing here and looking back down the valley immediately in front rises up in its lofty eminence, the Pic du Midi de Bigorre, 9,000 feet; on his left hand, Mount Perdu, 10,989 feet; and away far upon his right, towers aloft above its companions the almost inaccessible Maladette, 11,300 feet above the sea level. The snow-capped heads of these mountains, yielding to the heat of the sun's rays, distil their frigid coverings into streams of pellucid waters. As

A Month at Lourdes. 123

seen from this stand-point they look like so many rods of silver pursuing their devious courses down the mountain sides and rolling into the valley beneath. The neat little white churches which stud the valley and mountain-sides, their tiny spires pointing heavenwards; the sounds of the distant convent bells, as they ring out the "Angelus," added to the mellow-tinkling of the peculiar-shaped bells with which the several herds of kine and flocks of sheep are supplied, by the sounds from which in these fastnesses, the owners trace their whereabouts, all go to form one harmonious act of devotion to Him who so fashioned and made this glorious scene. Passing through the gap cut through the Tourmalet and shutting out from view the sterile hills of Gavarnie, we are brought into contact with a class of scenery which is superbly grand. The valley of the Campan is known to all readers of polite literature for its varied beauties. The Adour here taking its rise, soon swells into a respectable river, and the waters which contribute to its floods as they course down the mountains, form innumerable cascades which, heard amongst the foliage overshadowing their courses, is really delightful. As you descend the mountain towards the Grip you have need to brace your nerves. Hazardous as the ascent is from the valley on the other side of Tourmalet, the prospect of a speedy descent down the Grip valley is very alarming. Still I will say to all who visit Lourdes and can spare the time, see the valleys of Gavarnie and the Campan. If you are an admirer of nature you will here see her in some of her grandest habiliments. As we approached the village of Grip we met a number of shepherds going up to the mountains to take stock of the sheep, and shear them of their wool. Those light-hearted peasants were marching along in a military fashion, stepping out to the strains of two or three of the party who were singing one of the *chansons* of Beranger, or some other favourite poet, whilst the refrain was taken up by the remainder of their companions. How very like what one could witness in Ireland some forty years ago, when the industrious peasantry of the West trudged their way to their point of departure from the Green Isle for England, there to gather in the hay and corn harvests, so that they might earn a few pounds with which to pay the rent of their little homesteads. They too,

A Month at Lourdes.

like the peasantry of the Pyrenees, were accustomed to march to the lively airs of their country, when played for them by some piper or fiddler. We reached Bagneres de Bigorre, and found the place so crowded with visitors that our host of the Hotel de France could only provide us with food under his roof, and we had to find lodgings in another establishment. Unlike Bareges, Bagneres de Bigorre is a considerable town, having well-shaded promenades in its streets. The town boasts of some 11,000 inhabitants, whose numbers are added to during the season by from 7,000 to 9,000 visitors, who come for the waters. Many strangers remain during the winter, for from its sheltered situation the temperature is higher than in other parts of the South of France. The female portion of the townspeople are constantly employed in making articles of ladies' attire from the fine wool brought from Spain; and here are the principal manufactories of the Crêpe de Bareges. But it is from its many and important mineral springs that the town derives its greatest profit. These number about fifty, and are of various health-giving qualities. Of all the mineral waters of

France, they approach nearest those of Baden-Baden, and persons of limited means, who dare not visit that expensive place, can, at a moderate outlay, spend a few weeks pleasurably at Bagneres de Bigorre. On one side of Mont Olivet the town raises its wooded eminence, whereon are arranged shady walks, and from which some good views of the country can be had. Behind Mont Olivet rises the lofty Mont Bèdat, upon whose towering summit stands a statue of the Mother of God, of pure white marble, and larger than life in its dimensions. This statue of the Virgin can be seen for many leagues around, and, viewed from the town, looks, in its blue canopy of the heavens, a magnificent work of art. Time pressing, I did not approach the statue, for the journey occupies from two to three hours; but I gave ready credence to those who had made the ascent, that the view from its base is really grand and noble. Bagneres de Bigorre has played its part in the wars of France. The English had the place ceded to them by the Treaty of Bretigny, and, being on the frontier of Spain, the Spanish, English, and French armies had many a bloody engagement around its fortifications, none of which now exist.

The churches of the Carmelites and their convents are very good buildings, particularly the new church, Mont Olivet, which is really a splendid erection. Entering this church the morning after our arrival, I saw his Lordship Dr. Moreno celebrating holy Mass at one of the side altars. The parish church of St. Vincent must have been a noble structure before the revolutionary Vandals of 1793 made an attack upon it and destroyed its western end. It is still a fine church and has many altars of richly sculptured marble. I saw a very touching scene at an early Mass in St. Vincent's Church. Before one of the side altars near the end of the church, resting upon a trestle, lay a coffin, in which was the body of a female. Around the bier was grouped a number of young women who were offering up their prayers, and chanting the responses during the Mass of Requiem. As the corpse was carried out from the church I observed four young females bearing a pall after the bier, on which were bunches of flowers and immortelles. The priest and acolytes walked before the sad cortège, reciting the prayers set apart by the Church for such occasions. The novelty of this mode of burial excited my curiosity and caused me to inquire into the antecedents of the person thus taken to the grave. I learned that she was a young girl who had a short time before come from Alsace to seek employment at the Casino in the town, and that she became a singer and dancer in that place. The rest of her history is soon told. The conscience-stricken girl awakened to her folly, and in a moment of temporary aberration, took a draught of poison. The Church, who welcomed her innocent soul into the fold at the baptismal font, now threw the shield of her prayers around the departed soul. From the appearance of the High Altar of St. Vincent's it was evident that some one of note also had passed away, and I was not surprised when, later in the morning, I saw a procession of clergy, wearing the sombre vestments used in Masses for the Dead, accompanied by cross-bearers and the choir of the church, proceed to a distant part of the town, to a house in which a man lay dead. They shortly afterwards returned to the church, chanting on their way the "Miserere." After placing the coffin upon a catafalque in front of the altar, a solemn High Mass was sung for the repose of the soul of the deceased Christian. The solemn strains of the choir as they sang the *Dies Iræ* were very impressive.

A visit to the marble works of M. Geruzet will well repay the trouble. In this immense manufactory are employed over three hundred mechanics and artists. The beautiful flesh-coloured marbles of the district are here seen in all their grandeur of stratification. The huge machinery by which columns of great size are turned out is on a gigantic scale. In the showroom are exhibited a selection of the several articles made in the establishment, with the cost of each affixed. Beautiful white marble altars, complete in every part, can here be had for the modest sum of forty pounds sterling. If any of my readers are thinking of making a votive offering to some struggling priest who is attempting to beautify the temple of the Most High, let him give an order to M. Geruzet, who will send an altar to him. No one need be apprehensive of undue advantage being taken, for M. Geruzet is a man above suspicion, and he is also the local agent for Coutts and Co., bankers at London.

Visitors to Bagneres de Bigorre cannot but be

pleased with the extensive and beautiful display of flowers which are to be seen there. I noticed that in most parts of the Pyrenees flowers were not so abundant as the sunny nature of the climate might lead one to expect; but at Bagneres de Bigorre, there is a system of irrigation in action which abundantly supplies the gardens of the place with water from the Adour, and hence the floral productions of the town are rich and plentiful. This system of irrigation is almost self-acting by means of locks placed upon the river, and the waters are conveyed by conduits to all parts of the town, hence the non-necessity of making reservoirs, or using pumping machinery.

Having spent a very enjoyable time at Bagneres de Bigorre I was prepared to leave for Tarbes, *en route* for Paris, as my time of vacation was nearly expired, but yielding to the persuasion of my companions, especially to the clerical head of the party, I agreed to return to Lourdes for the night, and then start for home next day. Horses being put to, our carriages rolled along the streets, the drivers making the clear air resound to the sharp click of their whips. After a drive of two hours and a half through a pleasant and fertile country, we once more found ourselves under the shadow of Our Lady's Church at Lourdes.

CHAPTER VIII.

Thunderstorm at Lourdes.—The National Pilgrimage.— Numerous Miracles.—An Irishman's Faith in the Blessed Virgin.—A Miracle on Board an Atlantic Steamer in Mid-Ocean.—Pius IX. sends the Golden Rose to Lourdes.—Irish Prelate Pilgrims at the Grotto.—Return Homewards.—Tarbes.—Limoges : its Churches. — Issoudun. — Paris. — Versailles.— Rouen.—Jean d'Arc.—Dieppe.

AUGUST 18TH.—As mentioned in the last chapter, we came back to Lourdes this evening from Bagneres de Bigorre. Fortunately for us we arrived a couple of hours before the outbreak of a fierce thunderstorm which, had it overtaken us amidst the mountain passes, would have been very unfortunate for some of the female portion of the party. At Lourdes the noise of the thunder, as peal followed peal, was really terrifying to hear. Coming down the several valleys and gorges, the sound as it reverberated from hillside to hillside showed how fiercely the war of elements was being carried on. But, loud as roared the thunder, the brilliant light with which the mountains were illuminated, as the electric current shot around their sides and ascended to their highest peaks, was a truly grand and sublime spectacle to look upon and to admire. Few were abroad, for as the contending elements had exhausted themselves, and became once more reconciled, copious tears were shed, as is the case in human quarrels. The noise of the torrent, which soon swelled the floods in the Gave, helped to compose the affrighted people into peaceful slumbers.

August 19th.—Early on the morning of this day the shrill screams of the railway whistles proclaimed the fact that an unusual number of trains had arrived at the station, and soon the streets began to fill with the crowd of pilgrims, three thousand in number, who, amidst the fury of the storm, had travelled all night from distant Paris, that they might have the privilege of making their religious devotions at the blessed shrine of Our Lady of Nôtre Dame, at Lourdes. A little later on in the forenoon other trains arrived bringing a large number of pilgrims from the valleys and mountains of the Vosges. This day will ever be held in veneration at Lourdes. Now, indeed, did the Creator of the Universe show how powerful are the requests of the Blessed Mother of His Divine Son when pleading for her humble suppliants. After High Mass in the basilique, and when the thousands were assembled around the grotto, it was made known that a nun who had for many years suffered from a serious malady, depriving her of the use of her limbs, was miraculously cured and restored to perfect health. This miracle was followed by twenty-one others up to the afternoon of the 21st August, when the pilgrims left Lourdes to return to their distant homes. These wonderful manifestations of God's favour at the shrine of Our Lady were received by the multitude with acts of thanksgiving and joy. Such was the fervour of the faithful, that a Protestant gentleman holding an important official position under the Government became reconciled to the Catholic Church. From the 19th of August to the 18th of September no fewer than thirty-five persons of all conditions of society were miraculously cured of maladies, many of which had baffled the skill of the most eminent French physicians. I hold the names and addresses of the thirty-five persons referred to, which will be found in the succeeding chapter. It is none of my duty to discuss the authenticity of the many miracles which have been wrought at Lourdes. The opportunity of testing the genuineness of them has been brought home to the doors of the sceptics in hundreds of towns and villages throughout France and in other countries where the cured have resided. Although all who seek relief from bodily afflictions or other necessities do not obtain their requests at the shrine of Our Lady at Lourdes, none should hesitate to lay their petitions at the feet of the " Help of Christians," and leave the rest to God. Let me narrate two cases where faith in Mary's intercession proved singularly efficacious. An Irishman, who had visited Lourdes to seek restoration to health, by obtaining relief from a long endured infirmity, after a stay of some days experienced wonderful graces in his favour. After a time he left Lourdes on his return to Ireland in good health. Arrived at Bordeaux, and taking his passage for Liverpool, as the steamer sailed down the Garonne, his former malady re-visited him. As the vessel had to touch at Pauillac, some thirty miles down the river, the Irishman, strong in his faith in Mary's intercession, left the steamer, forfeiting his passage money, and when questioned why he would not continue his journey, said, "I came from Ireland to the shrine of Our Lady at Lourdes, to be cured, and I will go back to that blessed spot and *make the Blessed Virgin cure me!*" Back to Lourdes he went, and the faith which he held, and in his way so forcibly expressed, made him whole. Although some considerable time has since elapsed, no return of his malady has visited him. Again, a Catholic clergyman, an Irishman too, who had laboured amongst his countrymen for many years in America, and whose health had become enfeebled by the arduous duties of his ministry, sought relief from his afflictions at Lourdes, but did not find any mitigation of them. After some time this good priest took his return passage for America in one of the Cunard mail steamers. He had as fellow passengers two gentlemen, one a dignitary of the college of Maynooth, who was on a visit to America, and the other a gentleman who held, and still holds, an important official position under the government of the United States in France, and from whom I had the particulars, as follows: "From the time the steamer left Queenstown until she had reached mid-ocean the priest suffered intensely, never venturing out of his cabin. As I had heard that he had been to Lourdes I was much interested in him, and conversed often with him upon the many favours vouchsafed to persons who had visited there, but his sufferings were so great that he could not give his mind to much contemplation. On the eve of the feast of Our Lady of Mount Carmel, and the anniversary of the 18th apparition of Our Lady at Lourdes, I asked him if he knew what day it was, but he had forgotten it. I then spoke to him about the great festival of the morrow, and recalled to his mind the grotto of Our Lady at Lourdes. I then asked him if he would wish to have some conversation with a priest who was on board the ship. He expressed his desire to see the priest, who, when I informed him of the condition of his brother clergyman, went at once to his assistance. Next morning when we appeared at the table for breakfast the worthy priest came amongst us, his afflictions having most miraculously departed from him, and, as he declared, all through the intercession of Mary of Lourdes. He is still hale and strong, and grateful to the Blessed Mother of God for the great favours shown to him by God through her intercession."

A Month at Lourdes.

It need not be wondered that such extraordinary graces granted at Lourdes should have been heard of at Rome, or that the Holy Father's attention was directed to the sacred shrine. Hence it was that the Pope sent a special ambassador to Lourdes, in the person of the Right Rev. Monsignor Cretoni, Secretary of the Propaganda, charged with the duty of presenting to the church of Nôtre Dame the "Golden Rose." This beautiful and touching souvenir from his Holiness was received on the 15th of September, amidst great rejoicings, and now forms a distinguished object upon the high altar of the basilique. The Catholicity of Lourdes is seen in the congregating together of the faithful from all parts of the Christian world; and, as a matter of course, Ireland is almost daily represented by many of her zealous bishops, priests, and people. During the present year, the following prelates of the Irish Church paid a visit to Lourdes: the Most Rev. Drs. Gillooly, M'Evilly, M'Cormack, Dorrian, and M'Carthy. Lourdes only requires to be more fully known to increase the number of faithful pilgrims to the shrine of Our Lady in her favourite abode on the banks of the Gave. If anything I have written in this little work will induce visits to Lourdes, and by so doing, contribute to honour the Blessed Virgin, and obtain graces for those who journey there, any little trouble which I may have had in its composition will be amply repaid. Before taking leave of Lourdes, let me say that the citizens are now endeavouring to repay to the good and sainted Monsignor, the late curé of Lourdes, a portion of the debt which, when living, they withheld from him. A statue to the departed curé is about to be placed in front of the church which his zeal for the glory of God had brought so near completion, when his death removed him from the scenes amongst which he so long and so zealously laboured. One of the streets has had its former name removed, and that of the Venerable Peyramale affixed to it. Having taken a last fond look of the mountains, valleys, and woods of the Gave, and the beautiful church, convents, and ecclesiastical buildings, which the generous piety of the faithful have in such a short time raised up to the honour and glory of God, I took leave of the charming place in which I had spent the happiest weeks of my life, weeks which appeared as so many days, and directed my steps homewards.

A Month at Lourdes. 139

As I entered France upon its southern border, to vary my travels through the country I took a northern route upon leaving Lourdes. In doing this I traversed some of the most beautiful portions of that delightful country. The entire absence of weeds in the fields shows how carefully the land is cultivated. One could see more weeds in a mile's drive in Ireland or in England than could be seen in all France. The rotation of crops, as the farmers lay out their land, is very interesting to look at, and gives the country the appearance of a richly formed carpet. In straight lines of land of perhaps an acre each, you will see growing wheat, potatoes, hay, lucerne, maize, and green crops for feeding cattle. As the railway whirls you past, these various tinted crops present the appearance of a gorgeous ribbon, and the whole bespeaks a large measure of happiness of the people, to whose industry the charming prospective is due.

The first city of note met with on the road from Lourdes to Paris is Tarbes, twenty-four miles from the first named place. This city is the residence of a bishop, and is the great school in which the cavalry of France are trained. The Government has here a large breeding stud. Tarbes, like all the towns in the South of France, has a copious supply of pure water continuously running down its streets. On each side of the street there is a channel of say fourteen inches wide and four inches deep, through which the waters flow. The housewives bring their washing to the front of their houses, and, placing a board on end in the stream, wash their clothes. The water is also availed of to water the streets, and in carrying out this sanitary requirement I am sorry to say that, to my mind, the gallantry of France is found wanting, as the work is performed by females. Two women traverse the streets, supplied with wooden scoops having long handles, they lift up the water and throw it across the roadway; effectually laying the dust and cooling the heated atmosphere. Richard the Black Prince kept his court at Tarbes. Some fifty-four miles further, we come to Auch, where there is a splendid cathedral, whose imposing dimensions, as seen from the railway station, strikes the eye, for it is a grand object in the surrounding scenery. This cathedral dates back to the days of Clovis. The palace of the bishop is a magnificent building. Agen is next met, and this city, situated on the

A Month at Lourdes.

Garonne, has a canal which carries its waters over the river upon a viaduct of twenty-three arches. Placed on a high hill, there is a colossal statue of the Blessed Virgin. Agen is the centre of the great fruit gardens of France. Thousands of tons of fruit, preserved in their own juice, are yearly exported to all parts of the world.

The Garonne, being navigable by steamers of light draft from Agen to Bordeaux, facilitates the transit of produce to the seaside ports. The time occupied in going down the river is about eight hours, but owing to the strong current twelve hours are required to reach Agen from Bordeaux. Limoges is the next city of note reached after Agen, and this is one of the finest places on this route. The noble churches which Limoges possesses are well worth the attention of travellers. Having broken my journey here, I had some time to look about me. The cathedral of St. Etienne is said to be the finest of its style in France; but the Church of St. Michel-aux-Leons arrests the notice of all comers. Standing upon the highest ground in the city, its lofty spire is lost in the clouds. This church takes its name from the huge lions, carved in stone, which are placed above the portico. In the church of St. Pierre, there is a stained-glass window over the high altar, of exquisite design, showing the death and coronation of the Blessed Virgin. Limoges was nearly destroyed by fire in 1864, and the houses since erected to replace those burned down are of a superior style to the more ancient buildings. Here it was that the Black Prince caused the massacre of 3000 men, women, and children, in consequence of being obliged to take the place by siege. Not far from Limoges is Issoudun, a place rendered remarkable by the many miracles wrought in the church of the "Sacred Heart of Mary." Numerous visitors come yearly to Issoudun to pay their devotions. The church has a lofty square tower, upon which is placed a marble statue of the Virgin Mother of God, and which, from its great size, can be seen for many miles around. We passed Poitiers, Orleans, etc., and ere the shades of evening set in, the gilded spires and domes of Paris broke upon the view. To a stranger visiting Paris for the first time, the scenes presented to his wondering observation are overpowering, for everything he beholds is so grand and so different from all other cities. The spacious Boulevards, the public

A Month at Lourdes. 143

buildings, the churches, and the appearance of the inhabitants, all combine to impress one with the conviction that this is the city *par excellence* of the world. My stay being necessarily short, it would be presumptuous in me to attempt a description of Paris. What time I had at my disposal enabled me to pay a visit to Versailles. In the palaces which are at Versailles, all that wealth and art could do to show how a nation provides for its rulers has been done. The grounds, picture galleries, halls of audience, and salons are grand. In the court in which the state carriages are kept, wonderful evidences of design and constructive skill are displayed. When I state that some of the vehicles have cost £3000, their grandeur and sumptuousness may be imagined. The *cicerone* who accompanied my party, in pointing out one of the carriages, said, "This is the one in which the Prince Imperial was taken to the Madeleine to be christened, and when he goes to Nôtre Dàme to be crowned Emperor he will use the same one." Napoleonism evidently has a deep hold upon the affections of the French people. A visit to Versailles is worth the entire expense which might be incurred in a journey from this country.

As you pass from Paris to Versailles, you see the buildings in the Champs de Mars, in which the world's great fair of 1878 will be held. The extent of ground covered by the Exhibition buildings is considerable. The Seine at Paris is of great breadth, and when I mention that the Exhibition buildings are placed upon both the banks of the Seine, and that a bridge is being constructed by which each portion of the building will be connected, some idea may be formed of the hugeness of the structure. Most of the Exhibition buildings are of a permanent character, and are very handsome to look upon.

Leaving Paris for Dieppe, the country traversed is very fine. The abundance of timber growing upon the land gives the landscape a warm look, and the many ruins of ancient castles met with show how well their Norman possessors fortified their places of abode. Rouen, with its numerous churches should be seen. Here it was that the heroic Maid of Orleans, Jeanne d'Arc, was basely given up to the brutal English soldiery by the pusillanimous monarch, Charles VII., upon whose head she placed the crown of France. The young Shepherdess of Domrémy conceived the idea of rescuing her

A Month at Lourdes. 145

country from a foreign yoke, and when by her enthusiasm she had roused her countrymen and conquered the invaders, the poltroon, who had reached the throne by her superhuman exertions, stood calmly by whilst his benefactress and his people's saviour was being burned at the stake. Rome will soon do justice to the memory of the Shepherdess of Domrémy, for I believe a process is going on which will secure for Jeanne d'Arc, a place in the long roll of heroic women who have fought and died for the faith.

Dieppe now reached, the last scene of my travels upon French soil is about to close. This city is of historic fame, and it still possesses objects most worthy of the visitor's attention. I was very much struck with the Cathedral of St. Jacques. At six a.m., I had the privilege of attending Benediction of the Blessed Sacrament, and, at that early hour, of also hearing a sermon preached after the service. The church of St. Jacques is being restored, and when the work will be completed, the ancient glories of the sacred edifice will once more be seen in all their grand proportions. Dieppe has a considerable shipping business. The merry fishwives as they trudge from the harbour with their panniers of fish strapped upon their shoulders, and the high cauled caps of pure white, with their various-coloured kirtles, are a picturesque sight to look upon.

In the forenoon I sailed from Dieppe. As the two massive crucifixes on either side of the harbour gradually faded from my view, I could not forego the feeling of wishing peace and happiness to the country through whose hills and valleys I had rambled with so much pleasure and profit.

As all sublunary matters must have an end, so have my "Vacation Rambles in Southern France." No one is more conscious of the many imperfections in my descriptions of persons, scenery, and places contained in my narrative than I am myself; but I trust that those who have followed me in my travels, will have derived some little pleasure from perusing this work, and in their charity will overlook the many shortcomings which they may find in it.

CHAPTER IX.

Presentation of the Golden Rose by Pope Pius IX.—Interesting Ceremony.—Speeches of the Archbishop of Rheims, and the Papal Delegate.—Pius IX. and the Water of Lourdes.—Details of the Numerous Miraculous Cures.—Appendix.

THE Pope sent, by the Italian pilgrims, who arrived at Lourdes on the 15th September, 1877, as an offering to Our Lady's Shrine, a "Golden Rose Tree." This elegant work of art is divided into several small branches, on which are three full-blown roses in the midst of leaves of gold! A fourth is just commencing to unfold its beauties; and there are six charming buds. This rose tree rests in a large vase, skilfully and delicately worked with silver and gold, ornamented with emeralds and precious stones, and with bas-reliefs, where are seen the Eucharistic corn and wine, and two sweet adoring statuettes of angels, who hold in their hands—one the Anchor of Hope, the other the Archiepiscopal Cross.

This Rose, which was presented to Pius IX. by the Confraternity of Our Mother of the Sacred Heart of Issoudun, was sent by the

Holy Father to the Virgin Immaculate of Lourdes as a testimony of his love for the Mother of God. It is placed upon the High Altar of the basilica, at the feet of the Crowned Virgin, under the Golden Palm which the Pope sent a year ago. The Italian pilgrims arrived at Lourdes on the 15th of September, and consisted of sixty-three persons, many of whom were ecclesiastics. Monsignor Cretoni, Domestic Prelate of His Holiness, came with the pilgrims. On Sunday morning, before celebrating the pilgrims' Mass, the Monsignore expressed the feelings the pilgrims had experienced in setting foot on the soil of France, whose faith and charity they admired so much. He dwelt upon the joy they had felt on arriving at Lourdes—" Lourdes, nestled amongst picturesque mountains and delightful valleys ! A new Eden, where they had found a new Eve—Mary!" He reminded the pilgrims that they had come to render homage to Our Mother of Lourdes, in the name of Pius IX. and Catholic Italy ; to pray for their much loved Pontiff, for the Eternal City, and for their dear country, oppressed by the impiety of the revolution. Nothing could have been more graceful, elegant, touching, and eloquent than the harmonious Italian language, as it flowed from the lips and from the heart of the amiable and pious prelate. At the conclusion of the Mass, Monsignor Cretoni, on his knees before the altar, his arms outstretched with love towards the image of the Holy Virgin, presented to Our Mother of Lourdes a large and magnificent Silver Heart—symbol of the hearts He came to consecrate to her. He implored her to cast from the heights of Heaven a glance of love and grace upon her children, prostrated before her, in that place to her so dear. He prayed to her by her name so sweet, "Immaculate." "All the world," he continued, "come and bow the knee *here*, at the foot of thy throne! Thy well-beloved children of Italy, nurtured with their mother's milk in infancy, and reared up in constant devotion to thee; amongst them thou hast confided thy house of Nazareth, and they will ever put their trust in thee. On this day, sacred in honour of thy dolours, they mingle their tears with the tears of their Holy Mother, and seek to obtain a blessing and benediction for their souls, for the Pope, for Italy, and for the Church!" The evening ceremony was most solemn. The pilgrims assembled at the grotto, where they placed the Rose Tree of Gold. They march in procession to the basilica, singing the "Ave Maris Stella" and the Litany of Loretto. They are received in triumph in the church by the priests and servers, who sing the hymn of Pius IX., "Glory to the Universal Pontiff." His Grace the Archbishop of Rheims represented on this solemn occasion Monsignor the Bishop of Tarbes, who was absent from his diocese. He received on his knees the splendid offering of Pius IX., kissing the Rose at the same time.

The Envoy of the Pope, Monsignor Cretoni, then delivered in the harmonious Italian tongue, the thoughts of his pious heart. He spoke of the branches of the rose, queen of flowers by the delicacy of its form, the variety of its colour, and the sweetness of its perfume. He exalted her whom the Church terms the Mystical Rose, who condescended to appear with roses to the little peasant girl—that Mystical Rose who is Queen of Angels, the glory of the Church, of the earth, and of Italy. "Pius the IX. (he said), in sending a rose to the Immaculate Virgin at Lourdes, testifies that she is the most exalted of all creatures and the most dear to his heart. He thus shows also his veneration for this illustrious sanctuary. Formerly the Popes sent roses to crowned heads, great personages who had rendered signal services to the Church. They also sent them to the most renowned sanctuaries in the world. For example, Gregory XIII. to Our Mother of Loretto, and Paul V. to Saint Mary Major. Rejoice, then, venerable guardians of this glorious sanctuary! Pius IX. throws a new lustre over it to-day by sending this Golden Rose! Let us rejoice, well-beloved brothers of Italy and France. Let this precious gift revive our hopes! The rose is the flower of spring time. Winter—the winter of the Revolution—desolates everywhere the Catholic nations! But this rose, sent by the Pope to the Immaculate Virgin, is the sign of a new spring-time, which God will yet give to His Church and faithful people." This allocution visibly moved and melted the feelings of the whole assembly. Monsignor Langénieux rose to respond. He congratulated the Envoy of the Holy Father on having expressed with so much grace and force the sentiments which stirred the heart of the Pontiff. He said : " Pius IX. particularly and especially loves Our Mother of Lourdes, and his preference is both natural and just. It is here that the Immaculate Virgin has provided remedies for the evils which desolate the age, that pride which glorifies man, that materialism which classes him with the brute, that revolutionary spirit which says science and knowledge are all-sufficient. Pius IX. had prepared a remedy by the proclamation of the 'Immaculate Conception.' The Virgin appeared at this grotto to confirm the word of the Pope, and prepare the dogma of his Infallibility! Mary Immaculate, manifested to the world, affirms at once both the fall and the grandeur of man. She is the glory of humanity! Secondly, Pius IX. has testified, as the Envoy of the Pope has said so well, that the rose is the sign of the spring-time of hope. The heart of Pius IX., so thoroughly French as it is, sends us this hope with the Golden Rose, offered to a French Madonna. The Immaculate Virgin of Lourdes will save France, and by saving France will save Italy and the Papacy! Pius IX., we are assured of it, will take part in that triumph. Like that heroine of France, whose image I love to contemplate in the grand Cathedral of Rheims,

Pius IX., after having suffered the pain, will also share in the honour."

Doctor Seccarelli, physician to Pius IX., in the summer of 1877, obtained leave of absence to enable him to visit the grotto at Lourdes. He gave, with much joy, good news of the Pope's health. Rheumatism, which prevented his walking, caused him some pain when he moved about. Nevertheless, the pious Pontiff said Holy Mass every day, which of necessity inconvenienced him much. He added that Pius IX., by giving an example of obedience to the physicians, submitted to their treatment. At last, finding their remedies were useless, he renounced them. The Pontiff said, smilingly, "I only wish to use the oil of the Holy Virgin, the water of Lourdes." Each day He made, with this water, the sign of the Cross upon the paralysed limb, and the evening before the departure of the physician, Pius IX. received 400 bottles of the Lourdes water of the grotto, which he delighted in dispensing to the sick. A Cardinal, on wishing for two bottles of it, was answered by the Pope's Chamberlain, "You must wait till I have given an account of the water to the Holy Father."

The grotto has been much improved by the Fathers in charge. A handsome railing is placed in front, and large stands, which hold some 200 candles, are continually burning before the statue of Our Lady. Outside the grotto the space taken in from the Gave is covered with a composition which keeps the ground smooth and clean, whilst along the river a wall of granite is fixed, on the land side of which there is a ledge which serves as a seat. There is also on the south side of the grotto a rustic pulpit, from which the various pilgrims are addressed by the pastors who accompany them from their homes. There is a supply of candles kept close to the grotto, of which pilgrims can purchase and make an offering at the shrine. The gates of the grotto are closed each night at ten o'clock, but many linger about the place praying and drinking at the fountain.

August 20th.[*]—Madame Stéphanie Deperne religieuse of the Christian Education Society of Loos-lez-Lille (Nord), aged thirty-three years, suffered from chronic rheumatism for seventeen

[*] The cures here given are translated from the "Annales de Lourdes," for August and September, 1877.

years. The doctors said she might be relieved, but not cured. Carried to the basilica, she received Holy Communion, supported by her mother and sister. She was taken down to the grotto, where she remained praying to the Holy Virgin for a considerable time. Having made a vow to the Blessed Virgin, she was carried to the bath in which she stayed for a while. She came out, her rheumatism except in one foot had vanished; after a second bath all the pains had left her. For the whole of the day and night she remained at the grotto, charitably assisting others to partake of the bath and water of the grotto. Half an hour after this first miracle, Mrs. Lefevre, (née Lambert), a widow, aged sixty-five years, finding herself helpless upon the death of her husband, was admitted into the Hospice of Charity at Paris. From infancy she had suffered from a disease in one knee; and during the past year she could only walk with crutches. She kept her bed all last winter; her health was somewhat better in spring; she came with the pilgrims, having procured a "free ticket" for the journey; she goes into the bath, and is immediately cured.

Madame Augustine Quillé of Gien (Loiret),

suffered during the past eight years. During the last two years, her limbs had been paralyzed. She tried the mineral waters of Bourbon l'Anhambault, which only aggravated her disease. She suffered greatly coming from Paris to Bordeaux. At the latter place, the doctor accompanying the pilgrims sustained her strength with morphia and one of the priests administered extreme unction to her. Carried from the railway station at Lourdes, and placed in the bath, she felt a great sensation of health and force in all her body; she was able to walk out of the bath alone, and go up to the house of the missionaries, where all the particulars of her case were recorded.

Miss Mary Brugère, residing at 64, Avenue des Ternes, Paris, had been afflicted for more than two years with rheumatic gout, left behind by typhoid fever; she felt herself greatly relieved in the bath; the swelling in her hands entirely disappeared.

The Rev. Mother Marie-des-Anges, superioress of the Third Order of St. Dominick at Boulogne-sur-Mer, forty-eight years of age, had been a religieuse since she was fifteen years old. About three years ago a fracture of the knee-joint causing an effusion of matter—coupled with an enormous swelling. She suffered so much that she did not desire to go to Lourdes, but, yielding to a formal order of the Superior-General, she went, experiencing on the journey acute and grievous sufferings. The religious who accompanied her, plunged the patient into the bath twice without her experiencing any relief, but the third time she felt herself quite cured. The pain and swelling had left her. All those cures took place before the evening services in the basilica.

Sister Mary Joseph of the Holy Childhood of Mary, aged twenty-nine years, of the Convent at Thierville. She was afflicted with consumption, had got to the last stage of that insidious disease, dry cough, spitting of blood, and sleeplessness at night. These symptoms made the doctor say "that she would not be here long." She had kept her bed six weeks. The good religieuse had offered up her life as a sacrifice; she was not inclined to ask for its prolongation; obedience made it a duty that she should go to Lourdes. She obeyed, but with a certain fear, praying God's Will might be done. Since she thus prayed, she found herself not so ill, and was able to join in the Lorraine pilgrimage. She suffered much during the journey from coughing. She was taken to the bath, and when in the water felt herself constrained to pray that she might be cured, so as to become an instrument for the conversion of sinners. She was cured and became most active and earnest in praising God and His Blessed Mother, and in assisting the others who were afflicted.

August 21st.—Miss Mary Eugénie Bilon of Bertrimontier (Vosges), thirty-four years of age. At fourteen years of age she had a fall which injured her knee. She was compelled to use crutches; she came with the Lorraine pilgrimage. Going into the bath she was enabled to walk out of it without any assistance. She proceeded up to the house of the missionaries, and although her knee was not entirely healed, all pain had left her.

Mrs. Elizabeth Aubertin of Mayemont, aged forty-five years, had suffered for the past six years; after bathing, found all her pains (rheumatic) leave her.

Mrs. Marie Ernestine Chaperon, of St. Lumière-en-Champagne, aged thirty-six years, got a cold eight years ago, the result of which was a rupture in the right leg, which caused her to keep her bed for months. The disease was pronounced incurable. Plunged into the bath she was completely cured, and walked to the grotto and to the house of the missionaries.

Miss Marie Aubert of Tonnains, forty-eight years of age, had been subject all her life to ill-health, vomiting, heart disease, etc. Eighteen months ago her hands and legs became swollen. She was placed in the bath, and was immediately cured.

Germain Vigneroux, of the parish of St. Martin, L'Aveyron, nine years of age. When two years old, a tumour came in her knee, which developed into a sore, from which there was an issue; she walked on crutches, and after she had been plunged twice in the bath, she came out unassisted.

Justine Lepelletier, of Lille, thirty-four years of age, had suffered ten years rheumatic gout, which had settled in her legs, feet, and hands. The bones were ready to come through the flesh; the doctors declared her case incurable. Bathing three times in the bath, her legs and feet were completely cured and the swelling disappeared.

Miss Catherine Noëll d'Aurillac had suffered for five years from violent pulsations of the heart and pains in the stomach. After drinking four glasses of the water the palpitations of the heart ceased, and her appetite returned to her.

Victorine Loth, of Paris, 22, Avenue Friedland, aged twenty-seven years, suffered since last winter from gangrene, which wasted away her body and caused her great sufferings. After bathing she was completely cured.

August 22nd.—Mrs. Girard, of Niort, had been ill for four years with an internal cancer, attended with bleeding. She came from Niort by easy stages, because of her sufferings. In the bath she felt suffocated, and believed she was dying. She remained fifteen minutes in the water and, coming out of it, she cried, " I am cured !"

During the three days in which the National Pilgrimage from Paris was at Lourdes twenty-two miraculous cures were completed.

September 4th.—M. Fernand St. Elme, of D'Autry, thirty years of age, had suffered most cruelly from chronic rheumatism since he was sixteen months old. In consequence, his left side was paralyzed and incurable. Assisted by his uncle and a kind cousin he plunged into the bath ; he at once felt a powerful contraction in the stricken side, soon followed by a gradual feeling of warmth. He was astonished to find that the hand, awhile ago quite powerless and paralyzed, regained its power. The following day (5th) he was able, without any assistance, to follow in the procession and to take a second bath, which confirmed his cure.

Miss Louise Périnet, of Charenton-sur-Cher, seventeen years of age, had been tormented, since the preceding July, with a spasmodic affection of the throat, which caused her great suffering. She washed her throat with the water of the grotto, and was instantly cured.

Miss Susan Brunetière, of Fontenoy-le-Comte, 43, Rue Royale, aged twenty-three years, since she was five years old was afflicted with a spinal disease. She came, with much difficulty, with the Vendôme Pilgrimage, and, after bathing in the bath, came out perfectly restored to health.

September 5th.—Miss Mary Perraud, of Tizan (Vendée), twenty-one years of age, suffered since she was eight years old with a disease of the spine and hip-joint. She was admitted to the Hospital for Incurables at Laroche-sur-Yon. She came to Lourdes, and could only walk with difficulty upon two crutches. After a bath she discarded her crutches, and after a second one she was perfectly restored to the use of her limbs and to good health.

Miss Gertrude Schass, aged twenty-one, of 19, Grafton Street, London, suffered from phthisis since she was two years old. After several baths, her malady had completely left her.

September 7th.—Madame Josephine Gastey of Demu (Gers), thirty-two years of age, was afflicted with neuralgia and frequent hemorrhages. The doctors abandoned all hope of her recovery. She was advised to try the mineral waters of Bagneres de Bigorre, but she came with her husband to Lourdes. She washed and drank of the waters of the fountain, and was suddenly cured.

September 14th.—Miss Mary Daniel de Beaumont Périgord, aged twenty-two years, had been afflicted for several years with a swelling in the knee, which the doctors despaired of curing. When in the bath she experienced an intense shock of cold, followed by a gradual warmth. She came out of the water healed, and, leaving her crutches behind her, joined in a procession to the church.

Madame Mathilde Sieurac, of Lezat (Ariége), aged twenty-nine years, was seized on the 9th of October, 1876, with a cerebral bleeding, followed by paralysis of the left side. The left foot was twisted round. On leaving the bath, her foot returned to its natural position, and she walked unassisted.

September 17th —Miss Marie Nougués, of 121, Rue St Michel, Toulouse, aged twenty-four years, was attacked eighteen months ago with a severe disease in the stomach. The doctors gave her up. Arrived with the pilgrimage from Villefranche, she was carried to the Basilica, where she Communicated, was then brought down to the bath in a carriage, and dipped into the water whilst covered with perspiration. After a moment of oppression, she felt herself cured! She then walked to the grotto, where she fell upon her knees to thank Our Blessed Lady, and then ascended the steep road to the basilica. She wrote from Toulouse on the 20th of September, that her cure had caused a great sensation, and had been productive of much good.

September 18th.—Miss Gabrielle Loiseleur, of Chinon, residing at the Priory of St. Louan, aged twenty-four years, was afflicted since eight years old by an affection of the hip-joint and of her spine; she could not walk without crutches; she accompanied the pilgrims from Tours. She went into the bath and was cured.

Madame Julia Renard, of Tours, afflicted since sixteen years old with rheumatic gout—suffering more especially for the last two years—felt all her pains leave her whilst in the bath.

Madame Guerrier, of Beaume (Côte d'Or), had been suffering from paralysis of the lower half of her body. She was carried to the basilica, where she heard Holy Mass and received Holy Communion seated in a carriage. Immediately she received Holy Communion she went upon her knees, and after Mass raised herself up, and unaided taking the arm of her husband, she walked to the grotto, a considerable distance. Madame Guerrier's husband is a magistrate at Beaume.

M. Guillet, Archpriest of Niort, in giving an account of the pilgrimage from Poitiers, mentions the cure of Madame Gerard, and says: "This cure was the immediate occasion of much joy to a foreign lady in our pilgrimage. Her husband, an officer, witness with her of the miracles, said at once, 'I came here for curiosity; now I am *convinced* and *believe !*'"
M. Guillet writes further, stating that the little girl, Susan Servant, who lay in her bed for two nights at the grotto, and whose case excited so

much sympathy, has, since her return home, been perfectly restored to health.

September 24th.—Sister Rosalie, of the Congregation of St. Joseph, at Lyons, had been suffering from consumption and pains in her knees for three years. She was brought to Lourdes by the pilgrims from Rodez. She walked with extreme pain to the grotto. Having been placed in the bath, her pains became most agonising, and she requested the sister who was with her to lift her out. In obedience to the sister she once more goes into the water, after remaining in which for a few minutes, she finds herself cured, walks out of the water, joins in the procession to the Basilica singing the "Magnificat."

Many other most extraordinary cures were effected at the grotto of Lourdes during the remaining months of the autumn, particulars of which are recorded in the "Annales de Lourdes," a very interesting publication issued monthly, which can be had by applying to the Rev. Superior of the Missionaries, Maison des Missionaires, Lourdes, Hautes de Pyrénées. The subscription for twelve months, post paid, is 3f. 50c., or 3s. annually.

APPENDIX.

ROUTES FROM GREAT BRITAIN AND IRELAND TO LOURDES.

BEFORE leaving home, travellers would do well to bear the following particulars in mind. Take as small a quantity of luggage as you can possibly do with, and so escape much annoyance and many impositions. Provide a sufficient supply of soap, brushes, etc., for your toilet, as these articles are not supplied by hotelkeepers. Take a good-sized umbrella, of white material, so as to escape from the inconvenience of the sun's rays, and be sure to bring with you a good field-glass, as by so doing you will enjoy the grandeur of the scenery to be met with in the Pyrenean mountains and valleys. Change your English money into French coins, as in many places you will find it difficult to get shopkeepers and others to understand the value of English money.

The regulations which are laid down for the hiring of cabs, etc., are very stringent and are quickly put in force by the police if violated. Each conductor is bound to give the hirer of his vehicle a ticket, upon comparing which with the printed card, placed in the coach, etc., the correct fare can be easily ascertained. Choose the best hotels at which to stay, as the difference in charges betwixt first and second class hotels is very trifling, and is more than covered by the superior accommodation which will be provided for you. It is not necessary that you should have all meals at the hotel at which you may be staying, but it is requisite before leaving your hotel in the morning to inform the landlord of your intention not to be back for dinner, etc. At most of the hotels the cost of attendance is included in the bills; but where this is omitted, one half-franc a day is held to be sufficient for the services given.

A Month at Lourdes. 167

For such as wish to reach Lourdes from London, any of the routes from Dover, Folkestone, or Newhaven to Paris may be selected, according to taste or other considerations. The traveller can reach Lourdes from London, *viâ* Paris and Bordeaux, in twenty-four hours, and at or about a cost of, say, for first-class, £4 7s. 4d.; second ditto, £3 5s. 6d. ; and third ditto, £2 8s. 0½d.

There are steamers sailing from London, Liverpool, Glasgow, and Dublin for the City of Bordeaux, by which Lourdes can be reached in about three days; and as the passengers are found in everything in the way of food, except wines and spirits, which are to be had on board at reasonable prices, those who have time and are not afraid of sea-sickness will find an excursion by sea a most enjoyable way of reaching Bordeaux. The vessels which sail from Dublin and Glasgow are only occasional traders, and have not such good accommodation for passengers as those sailing from Liverpool have. Two lines of steamers leave Liverpool regularly for Bordeaux. The Pacific Company's Royal Mail steamers, each alternate Wednesday; and James Moss and Co.'s steamers, which sail weekly. The rates of passage by the Pacific Company's vessels are: first-class, £5 5s.; second-class, £3 3s., with the option of returning first-class for £8. By James Moss and Co.'s steamers, the rates are: first-class, £4, return, £7; second-class, £2 10s.

The railway fares from Bordeaux to Lourdes are: first-class £1 7s. 3d.; second, 19s. 5d. ; and third, 15s. 2d.—the time taken about eight hours. If when at Bordeaux, and time permit, the Circular Tickets, issued by Messrs. Cook and Sons, which cost £3 0s. 1d., will enable the traveller to see some of the most beautiful places in the Pyrénées, namely, Agen, Montauban, Toulouse, Montrejeau, Tarbes, Bagneres de Bigorre, Lourdes, Pierrefitte, Pau, Bayonne, Dax, and Arcachon, allowing twenty days for the tour.

If visitors to Lourdes wish to return to Paris by a different route than by Bordeaux, they can do so by travelling to Agen, Limoges, Issoudun, and Orleans, and thus have an opportunity of seeing some beautiful scenery. Tours, the birthplace of St. Martin, uncle to the Apostle of Ireland, is easily reached by this route. Coming from Paris to Lourdes, *viâ* Bordeaux, I would advise the traveller to choose the route by Pau, instead of that by Tarbes, as by doing so the pics and valleys of the Gave can be seen to great advantage, besides the traveller will have a good view of the churches and Calvary at Betharram. The difference in time and cost is very trifling.

I don't know that there is anything upon which I could be of advantage to notice, as all intelligent travellers will readily enough find the means of easily filling up any omissions which I may have made.

THE END.

www.ingramcontent.com/pod-product-compliance
Lightning Source LLC
Chambersburg PA
CBHW020313170426
43202CB00008B/588